Praise for
For the Love of God

"Religion only leaves us empty and longing for more. What we really need is a love affair—a heart-gripping, world changing, head-over-heels falling for Jesus. Through her personal story as well as encouragement and spiritual insights, Jenny Lee Sulpizio guides us to the place where we truly belong . . . the arms of a God who has been waiting for us all along."

   —**Holley Gerth,** best-selling author of *You're Already Amazing*

"Jenny remembers going to church and wondering what the big deal was, wandering from her childhood faith, searching for something more—only to return and find exactly what she'd been looking for! Now in her warm, witty, down-to-earth way, Jenny welcomes other women to rediscover the love of God and experience again—or maybe for the first time—the power of His forgiveness, healing, and grace."

   —**Christin Ditchfield,** author of *What Women Should Know about Facing Fear*

"*For the Love of God* is a fresh, inviting look at the nuts and bolts of faith—and what it means to call yourself a Christian. Without a trace of preachy banter, reading this book makes you feel like you sat with Jenny for a cup of good coffee ~~~ ~ ~~~ a glimpse of the stunning Savior.

   —**Gari Meacham,** ~~~~~~~~~~~~~~~~~~~~~~ ~d *Moments,* and *Truly* www.garimeacham

"Pour yourself a fresh cup of coffee, settle into your favorite spot on the sofa, and meet Jenny Lee Sulpizio. By the end of the first chapter, you'll feel like you've known her all your life. Jenny is the real deal—funny, authentic, and relatable—and she doesn't shirk the tough questions or sugarcoat her story. Instead, her humor and refreshing candor will put you instantly at ease.

"Whether you're a seasoned believer or lingering tentatively on the fringe of faith, *For the Love of God* offers you a simple but powerful invitation: come closer to God. By the time you turn the final pages, you'll find yourself with renewed inspiration and a wealth of resources to guide you toward the next step on your spiritual journey, whatever that may be."

—**Michelle DeRusha,** author of *Spiritual Misfit: A Memoir of Uneasy Faith*

"Jenny Sulpizio is, indeed, a woman who is willing to share her journey, her struggles, and her testimony to help others in their spiritual walk. With her characteristic humor and grace, Jenny unwraps the elements of faith and gives us a practical guide to stepping deeper into the Mystery. With helpful reading assignments and growth-provoking questions, *For the Love of God* is a must-read for anyone who desires a rich God-life."

—**Laura J. Boggess,** author of *Playdates with God: Having a Childlike Faith in a Grown-up World*

For the Love of God

FOR THE

LOVE

of

GOD

A Woman's Guide to
Finding Faith and Getting Grace

Jenny Lee Sulpizio

LEAFWOOD
PUBLISHERS

an imprint of Abilene Christian University Press

FOR THE LOVE OF GOD
A Woman's Guide to Finding Faith and Getting Grace

LEAFWOOD
PUBLISHERS
an imprint of Abilene Christian University Press

Copyright © 2014 by Jenny Lee Sulpizio

ISBN 978-0-89112-657-7

Scripture quotations, unless otherwise noted, are from The Holy Bible, New International Version®, NIV® Copyright © 1973, 1978, 1984, 2011, by Biblica, Inc.® Used by permission. All rights reserved worldwide.

Scripture quotations marked AMP are from the Amplified Bible, Copyright © 1954, 1958, 1962, 1964, 1965, 1987 by The Lockman Foundation. Used by permission.

Scripture quotations marked CEV are from the Contemporary English Version® Copyright © 1995 American Bible Society. All rights reserved.

Scripture quotations marked ESV are from The Holy Bible, English Standard Version® Copyright © 2001 by Crossway, a publishing ministry of Good News Publishers. All rights reserved.

Scripture quotations noted *The Message* are taken from *The Message*. Copyright 1993, 1994, 1995, 1996, 2000, 2001, 2002. Used by permission of NavPress Publishing Group.

Scripture quotations marked NASB are from the New American Standard Bible® Copyright © 1960, 1962, 1963, 1968, 1971, 1972, 1973, 1975, 1977, 1995 by The Lockman Foundation. Used by permission.

Scripture quotations marked NKJV are from the New King James Version® Copyright © 1982 by Thomas Nelson, Inc. Used by permission. All rights reserved.

Scripture quotations marked NLT are from the Holy Bible, New Living Translation, Copyright © 1996, 2004, 2007 by Tyndale House Foundation. Used by permission of Tyndale House Publishers, Inc., Carol Stream, Illinois 60188. All rights reserved.

Scripture quotations marked NLV are from The New Life Version Bible © Christian Literature International.

Published in association with the Seymour Agency, 475 Miner Street Road, Canton, NY 13617.

Library of Congress Cataloging-in-Publication Data
Sulpizio, Jenny Lee.
  For the love of God : a woman's guide to finding faith and getting grace / Jenny Lee Sulpizio.
    pages cm
Includes bibliographical references and index.
ISBN 978-0-89112-657-7 (alk. paper)
1. Christian women--Religious life. I. Title.
BV4527.S85 2014
248.8'43--dc23
                                                                        2014033857

Cover design by Beca Clifton
Interior text design by Becky Hawley Design

For information contact:
Abilene Christian University Press
1626 Campus Court
Abilene, Texas 79601
1-877-816-4455
www.leafwoodpublishers.com

14 15 16 17 18 19 / 7 6 5 4 3 2 1

Table of Contents

"To fall in love with God is the greatest of all romances; to seek him, the greatest adventure; to find him, the greatest human achievement."

—Augustine of Hippo

Acknowledgments

I must first thank God, who brought me on this journey, put the idea of this book in my head, and then laid the path to publication out in front of me. This is for Him, and I am grateful beyond measure, and so humbled by this blessing.

Thank you to Leafwood Publishers and their team for believing in the message of this book. My heartfelt appreciation to Gary Myers, Leonard Allen, Mary Hardegree, Philip Dosa, Seth Shaver, Ryan Self, Lettie Morrow, and Duane Anderson.

A special "thanks" to Dr. Steven Crane, Paul and Laurie Mondragon, and Caleb Breakey for their words of wisdom and godly counsel.

For Emily Wierenga and her beautiful words. You inspire me, friend.

For Brooke McGlothlin: Your friendship, encouragement, prayer, amazing launch skills (and love of all things '90s related) have meant so much to me over the past couple of years. You're simply the best. Thank you.

To Alle and Nate McCloskey of Finding Eden Media for all of their assistance, guidance, and dedication to this project and countless others. Blessed by you.

For Lindsey Hartz and the fabulous women comprising my launch team: Thank you, thank you, thank you for your support and efforts. You're an author's dream.

So much gratitude—as well as a ginormous hug—to each of the amazing women featured in this book, for their testimonies, their hearts, and their inspirational works. I am so blessed to call each one of you "friend": Joanne Kraft, Carey Scott, Tracy Steel, Natalie Chambers Snapp, Jennifer Dukes Lee, Hester Christensen, Laura S. Cabanillas, Kathy Howard, Heather R. Riggleman, and Stephanie Shott.

To my wonderful husband, children, friends, and family . . . thank you for the support you've given me to continually pursue this dream. I love you.

And finally, to you—the reader: May you finally understand the depth of His love and truly begin to grasp the magnitude of His grace. This is for you, friend.

Foreword

I am *that* girl.

You know, the one who sat on the hard pew of her father's church and planned to starve herself because she was angry at a hypocritical world.

Yeah, that one—who turned anorexic from the age of nine to thirteen because this institutionalized religion, it didn't make sense. It says one thing in the Bible, but the church—it does another. It pretends to get it, while talking about each other in hushed and reverent tones.

It wasn't until I was thirteen and dying, sixty pounds and purple with hypothermia, that I met Him for the first time.

This God that everyone was talking about.

And He wasn't like them. He wasn't like the church.

No, He was God, and He became a friend. He became a mother and a father and a brother and a holy Creator who put a tremble in my step. He was indescribable, and He sang over me.

The Bible says He sings over us, sisters, and you know? I heard Him for the first time that day, and I've heard Him ever since—the tender song of a God so in love with a people who don't see Him for all of their fears.

For the Love of God is God's love song, written down in book format for you. It's Zephaniah 3:17 in eleven thoughtful, well-resourced chapters that will pull you in like a pair of strong arms.

It's not just another Christian book. It's a book that speaks straight to the hurting, to the cynical, to the doubting amongst us. It's a book for those who've been hurt by the church, a book that longs to breathe life into dry bones.

It's a book for the world-weary, the messy, the broken. It's a book for everyone who hungers yet doesn't know where to find bread.

Join Jenny at the table. She is the real deal, friends. She's not here to give you lip service. No, she's here to say, "Yes, I've been there, and let me introduce you to a God you never knew existed—because He's been waiting. For you."

Waiting to lead you home.

All my heart,
e.

Emily T. Wierenga
www.emilywierenga.com

Author of five books, including the memoir *Atlas Girl: Finding Home in the Last Place I Thought to Look*

A Note to the Reader

Before we embark upon this adventure together (and prior to getting immersed in the message of this guide), I have to tell you girls something: I'm a little freaked out.

Does this sound odd? I mean, here I am, a Christian woman writing a whole book on the pursuit of God and all things holy, and I'm finding myself a tad bit anxious, a little apprehensive, somewhat nauseous, and yes, completely vulnerable.

I guess I've got some explaining to do.

See, I'm trying to condense *and* relay the greatness of God(!) into eleven chapters—and in a manner you, the reader, can relate to, understand, and want to pursue on a regular basis. Here I am, typing these words (in my pj's and slippers no less), attempting to inform you how the love of our heavenly Father can indeed change your life—and my anxiety is rising. My nerves? Present.

After all, who am I to write a book on faith? I don't have a degree in divinity, nor am I a theologian. Biblical scholars like Beth Moore and Kay Arthur have absolutely no clue as to who I am either. Rather, I'm a mom of three, a wife of one, and a daughter of the most-high King (Jesus) . . . and I happen to be a woman who has struggled with her faith throughout most of her life. Yep. I've ignored Christ and slighted God, I've wrestled with doubts and wallowed in shame—and have made plenty of mistakes along the way. In fact, in more ways than one, I'm fairly certain you and I might be a lot alike.

And that's why I've written this book.

Friends, the sole purpose of this text is to get you started (or restarted) on your walk with God—this journey with Jesus. It's about starting fresh . . . and starting over. Throughout it you'll find Scripture-based advice, testimonials, prescriptions for praise, and everything else you'll need in order to take those important first steps toward authentic faith.

It's not a how-to kind of book, because no one's path is quite the same; rather, it's a companion for the road ahead, a guide, if you will. It's meant to calm your fears, answer your questions, and reveal the grace you've been extended, along with the forgiveness you've been afforded. It's your introduction (or reintroduction) to our Savior and to God.

But before we dig in, I've got to tell you how much I've prayed for you in writing this book—how much I've begged God on your behalf to equip me with the right words to say in order to stir your soul to a place of action and understanding. Friend, from this day forward, your past is gone and your eyes need only look to the future, because this guide—well, it's focused on where you're going instead of where you've been. That's right. What you hold in your hands promises to offer hope, love, and encouragement . . . just as Jesus did.

I'm confident that the support you desire in forming a relationship with the Lord can be found in these pages, and I pray you'll learn to draw closer to Him by experiencing the unimaginable and unconditional love you were always meant to know.

This is for (and about) you, girl.

And it's for the love of God.

PART 1

Missing Out

"There's so much to experience, and so much we are missing out on by not believing."
—**Beth Moore,** *Believing God* **Bible Study**

Lost & Found

Bible thumper.

As a young adult, that was the last thing I ever wanted to be called. To read from the Bible, profess Christ, quote Scripture, and be in the Word?

Um, not cool.

I mean, who would want to hang out with me, and what kind of reputation would I get if I did those things? Besides, there'd be plenty of time to find religion, work on my faith, and get to know God, right? Because I'd already decided my life was going to be all about me: the clothes I wore, the men I wanted to date, the money I planned on making, and the fun I was going to have. Simply stated, there wasn't room for Jesus, and I guess you could say I was pretty hard-pressed to find time for God, too. Hey, having faith was great and all, but I was a girl who was much more concerned with what the inside of my closet contained rather than with what was taking place within my soul. I was too busy vying for attention in all the wrong places and spending all of my time consumed with the "things" around me.

God does love a good challenge, doesn't He?

I mean, why else would He transform a broken-down, potty-mouth, attention-starved, slightly dysfunctional woman like me and then ask her to write a book on faith of all things? And grace?

You've got to be kidding.

You see, from a young age, my introduction to church and all things holy never went over all that well. Sure, I "believed" in God and I knew about Jesus, but I was a kid who only attended church every so often (like on the big holidays) and, for me, well—the sermons were filled with a whole lot of talkin' (which intuitively made me want to do a whole lot of walkin'). I was pretty good at reciting prayers, but I had no relationship with God or His Son, Jesus Christ. Honestly, I didn't know I was supposed to. I didn't know it was my job to invite the Lord into every aspect of my life. Nor did I realize that I should be praying to and relying upon Him for help at all times. I didn't have a clue that I needed to share my gratitude and appreciation with my heavenly Father on a daily basis either. For me, it seemed as though the practice of getting to know God (and understanding this thing dubbed "religion") involved a bunch of rules I had no interest in pursuing.

I was a lost girl and didn't know it . . . for a really long time.

Friends, I'll venture to guess that you've picked up this book for the simple reason that you might be struggling as well. Maybe you're a gal in need of answers, but aren't quite sure of where to begin or how to go about it. Maybe you're a woman who's been to church before, glanced at the Bible a few times, and used prayer every once in a while . . . but find yourself unsure what to make of it, or how to feel that "closeness" you desire with your Creator.

Or maybe you've been broken down by the weight of this world, have nowhere else to turn, are feeling stuck and alone, and have found yourself here, reading this book—in need of a Savior.

Let me tell you—it's no accident.

You see, this book—the manual you hold in your hands—was written especially for you. Yes, you! Because so many of us have lost our way in this life we're living. So many of us have chosen (whether we've realized it or not) to exist separate from God and the teachings of Jesus Christ.

And it's just not working.

As you're already aware, I'm no theologian. But I am a woman called by God to write this guide—to help my fellow sisters figure out why seeking Him, why having a spiritual life immersed in Christ is the only way to go. Indeed, I'm a woman who can offer some pretty sound advice for anyone who's willing to listen.

So, am I a Bible thumper?

I guess it all depends on how you look at it. Do I love Jesus and praise God for every blessing (and through every trial)?

I do.

Do I believe in the salvation that's been given to me through the death and resurrection of Christ Jesus?

One hundred percent.

Will I profess my heavenly Father's name, and defend His honor?

Every. Single. Time.

So, am I a Bible thumper?

I guess you could say I am.

And you know what? There's nothing like it . . . nothing better . . . nothing greater.

Indeed, there's nothing cooler.

> *I've never known anyone to come to Christ and ever regret it.*
> —**Rev. Billy Graham**

You know what, friends? Maybe it's time to cast those fears aside, kick those doubts to the curb, and awaken to what this life (as well as the next) can really offer. Maybe it's time to finally give God a chance.

Rise and Shine

Waking up? Sometimes it's not all that easy.

Like in that moment where you've reached the peak of relaxation, nestled snuggly in your warm sheets, the comforter cradling your every inch, and all is seemingly right with the world, and then it happens. The ever-dreaded alarm clock sounds, beckoning you to get up and start the day. You're forced to rise (after a few hits on the snooze button), take a shower, find an outfit that fits and coordinates, get ready, and get going. It's off to work, or school, or maybe getting the kids ready for school. Day in and day out, this is your life.

But where's the meaning?

Where's the help you so desperately desire?

And better yet, where's God?

Life can be pretty tough at times and there's no "easy" button to help us figure it out either. Nor are we equipped with an autopilot, backup parachute, or other life-preserving device to assist us. Instead, we're subject to the twists, turns, hardships, and struggles this world has to offer. We are women attempting to control it all, on our own, separate from our Savior . . . and we're getting nowhere fast.

Many of us are unhappy.

Some of us are just plain miserable.

And the majority of us? Well, we're completely unaware of what we're missing out on.

But there's a better way.

Because there's hope.

Girls, consider this book to be your wake-up call—your opportunity to begin again. This is the time in your life where that uncomfortable feeling (the one that tends to accompany the unknown) is actually a good thing. No, make that a GREAT thing. This is the chance to

> God is always seeking you. Every sunset. Every clear blue sky. Every ocean wave. The starry host of night. He blankets each new day with the invitation, "I am here."
> **—Louie Giglio**

let go of your past and lay it all down: the burdens, the trouble, the pain, and the fears. This is where *you* get to know God.

But maybe we should explore why a relationship with Him is so important; why understanding the life and teachings of His Son, Jesus Christ, is vital; and why the pursuit of living authentically as a Christian is crucial. So, whether you're single, married, widowed, or divorced . . . whether you have children or are an empty nester, no matter what stage of life you're in or what circumstances you've dealt with in the past, this is the time to wake up. This is the time to seek a relationship with God. Friends, this is your opportunity to finally understand the depth of His grace and love by experiencing His presence in your life.

> I believe in Christianity as I believe that the sun has risen: not only because I see it, but because by it I see everything else.
> **—C. S. Lewis**

May I provide a disclaimer though?

Getting to know God (and accepting Jesus) doesn't mean life will suddenly become easier. It won't make those struggles go away, but it will make them bearable. It doesn't mean your problems

> *Don't turn away from God, precious sister. Don't harden your heart, or keep Him at arm's length either. For He bends down to hear you, He's always listening and He's always there.*
> —**Jenny Lee Sulpizio**

will be solved, but it means having Someone to face those challenges with. Girls, the relationship you're seeking is going to change the way you look at everything . . . and let me tell you, waking up will have never felt so comfortable, so freeing, or so good.

So, what do you say to ignoring that snooze button once and for all by embracing the call that's been pleading for your attention? What do you say to waking up to a life in Christ and all you've been missing out on?

The New Girl

Being the new girl—there's nothing fun about it. Not in the least. In those situations where we find ourselves amid different surroundings—be it a new job, home, town, or school—the uncertainty and lack of confidence that accompany such instances can be downright crippling. Isolation creeps in, fear takes over, and it's in these times when we feel lost. Alone.

I hate those feelings.

When it comes to being the new girl with this whole faith thing, it's no different. We're unsure what to ask, who to get answers from, or what steps we need to take first. We're in search of someone who can help, a person who understands the fragile place we're in, and where we're coming from. We're looking to find another who can relate to the way we feel.

Believe me; I get it.

Throughout this book, I plan on sharing the message of Christ and the Word of God with you in a number of ways. Ultimately, your salvation is between you and the Lord; however, my goal is to walk with you on this journey—to provide assistance in any way I can. I will share my testimony, my adventures in faith, and yes, even some of my mistakes. I will offer encouragement, insight, a few soapbox moments, and I'll be sure to send a number of thought-provoking questions your way as well. Oh, and I'll be inviting several of my friends to do the same. Because even though there's a ton of books out there on the topic of faith, and probably a few hundred on grace, this guide was written to meet you in the here and now, right smack in the middle of those doubts, unanswered questions, and issues you're bound to battle with as the new girl seeking God.

But that's not all.

My desire throughout this book is to present these topics as if you've never heard them before, all while appealing to those who have. So if you get confused, stop and contact me. If you read through this book and still have questions, please reach out because the point you're at right now—slightly hesitant but fairly curious, interested in God but not knowing how to initiate this pursuit—is delicate. It's raw. And it's such a crucial point in your quest for salvation.

Let's do this . . . together.

Getting Started

So what are the basics? I hate to call anything having to do with God's word "basic," because what's taken place over these past centuries is anything but. However, here's the gist, and the starting point from which we'll begin: Roughly two thousand years ago, God sent a form of Himself down to this earth to save us from our sins. And why? Well, it all began in a garden called Eden. It started with Adam and Eve, their disobedience toward God, and the great fall that took place. It was from that point on that man would forever know sin . . . and need a Savior.

That's right; the Messiah (Jesus) fulfilled a prophecy that dated back thousands of years. He came in the form of a baby, born to a virgin (Mary), in the humblest of beginnings. Jesus grew into a great teacher, a prophet who was able to heal, professed love to all, only to then be arrested, put on trial, beaten, and yes, crucified on a cross for blasphemy against the temple. His body was placed in a tomb and by the third day, He had risen, and rejoined our Father (God) in heaven a short time later.

His death wasn't normal by any means, because His self-sacrifice meant eternal salvation—it meant that you and I could (and would) be saved from our sins. Jesus died for us. He who knew no sin willingly took on ours. He gave His life in order to afford us grace and eternal paradise should we choose to accept it. He hung on that cross in place of you and me. He lived, He died, He rose, and one day, He's coming back again (Matt. 24:36–39).

But there's so much more to this story, girls. So much you have yet to know, to learn, and to absorb. There's so much I want to say . . . to tell you.

Indeed, this is just the beginning.

PART 2

Seeking … Searching

"Behold, I tell you a mystery: . . . in a moment,
in the twinkling of an eye, at the last trumpet . . .
we shall be changed."
—1 Corinthians 15:51–52 NKJV

CHAPTER 1

Finding Faith

For we walk by faith, not by sight.
—2 Corinthians 5:7 NKJV

Faith.

It seems as though everyone's talking about it these days. You hear phrases like, "Keep the Faith," and "Gotta Have Faith." Pastors and church members alike stress the importance of finding (and maintaining) faith. Book after book discusses the issues surrounding one's faith. But honestly, what does it *really* mean?

What is faith?

As I see it, biblical faith has lost its significance within our culture. It's a word that's been taken out of context, used loosely and without regard for its true, intended meaning. After all, you can place your faith in a lot of things that aren't necessarily spiritual, right? For example, I have faith that my husband will eventually learn to appreciate my crazed sense of humor. I have faith that one day my toddler son will stop using his potty training toilet for a

Cheerio receptacle, and I also have faith that in the not-so-distant future, my tweenage daughter will realize I'm the coolest mom on the planet and so deserving of her respect. Faith, as it applies to these particular instances, doesn't (necessarily) have anything to do with a devotion to God, or a genuine belief in Him. Rather, it's hoping, wanting, and probably a whole lot of wishful thinking on my part. I think it's fairly important not to underestimate the significance of this discipline—this belief—so allow me to share just a little bit about what faith means to me.

Biblical faith is believing and trusting in God. It's acknowledging His love, and the gift of eternal salvation He afforded each one of us through the sacrifice of His Son, Jesus Christ. Faith is a commitment; it's reading God's Word—the Bible (you know—that BESTSELLER?)—and interpreting/applying its message(s) to our lives. And finally, faith—as I see it—is a verb. It's to be professed by the tongue just as it is to be revealed by one's actions. It is to be worked upon just as often as it is tested. Faith is a gift by which God changes your heart. Simply stated—faith is *everything*.

> Faith is vitally important in the life of the Christian. It is by faith that you are saved; you are justified; cleansed, and look forward to the return of Jesus. Faith is where you please God, admit your dependence upon Him, and continually seek to rely upon Him and His grace. (Matt Slick, Christian Apologetics and Research Ministry)

Saved. Justified. Cleansed. Redeemed. You've got to admit: this whole faith thing sounds pretty amazing, right? But reading about it is one thing. Putting it into action? That's a whole other story. I mean, how does one "get" faith in the first place? What does it feel and look like? Where can it be found? And seriously, how does a person "*work*" on her faith?

Upon becoming a Christian, I hadn't a clue how I was supposed to locate this sort of devotion. And even though definitions like Matt Slick's provided me comfort, they

> *Faith doesn't have to be perfect to be strong.*
> —**Jessica Bowman**

still didn't show me the path I needed to take in order to initiate a genuine relationship with God, nor did they instruct me on how to rid my mind of the doubts that kept surfacing every time I thought about Him and His "love" for me. Besides, the act of "believing" is a pretty interesting concept anyways—placing your confidence in God, whom you are unable to see. God—the deity you might have only heard of and *occasionally* read about but certainly not a love you've *ever* experienced before.

One can't help but have doubts. One can't help but think: *Where is the proof that God exists? In order to really believe in something, shouldn't we be able to see it first?*

> *Making Jesus enough in your life opens your eyes to the way He sees the world. And it changes you.*
> —**Kristen Welch**

These seem like logical questions to ask and normal thoughts to have. But you know what I've realized? Our sight certainly can't be the *only* way we can firmly believe in something and hold it as truth, can it?

I mean, do we really need to *see* in order to believe?

For the general population, this appears to be the case. It's as if we need God—in all His glory—to descend from heaven, reveal Himself, maybe sit down for a quick latte and a round of twenty questions, pose for an Instagram shot, and then be on His way. We need proof He exists in order to justify the very idea of God to others . . . and yes, even to ourselves.

But why do we struggle, hesitate, and second-guess our Creator when the desire to know and have a relationship with Him is hard-wired within?

In her book, *Fed Up with Flat Faith*, author Kathy Howard discusses the desire God created in each one of us to connect with Him, describing it as "an intense longing that only the passionate pursuit of Him can satisfy."[1] Girls, do you know what she's saying here? Each of us is born with a craving, a thirst, an actual need to have a relationship with the Lord. However, most of us manage to find other things to feed such desires—things that draw us further away from the Lord. If you take a moment to think about it, you might be able to detect what you've placed in front of God in your own life. Maybe it's your job, your kids, your to-do list, your schoolwork, the annual shoe sale at Nordstrom's. Or maybe it's (dare I say) sex, drugs, money, or worse. Whatever it is, our souls are never completely satisfied because none of these things will ever make us content. They will never supply us with the inner peace we long to possess.

Not like He can.

> We pursue God because, and only because, He has first put an urge within us that spurs us to the pursuit. . . .
> The impulse to pursue God originates with God, but the outworking of that impulse is our following hard after Him.
> —A. W. Tozer

Girls, there is a void within each of our souls that can only be filled by the One who created us. When we ignore this craving or feed it with something else—something other than what it needs—well, it's no wonder it doesn't work.

And guess what: it's not supposed to.

Excuses, Excuses

Spiritual hunger is one thing. Making excuses as to why we're not feeding our souls is another. I'm a woman who has made plenty of excuses in my life, and when it came to finding my faith, let's just say I remained pretty consistent in doing so. You see, some of us—well, we just don't *want* to believe. No really. Many of us don't *want* to know there's a God. We don't *want*

> *And without faith it is impossible to please God, because anyone who comes to him must believe that he exists and that he rewards those who earnestly seek him.*
> **—Hebrews 11:6**

to hear about Jesus, His sacrifice, the cross, or the love that He has for us either; because for some of us, it's too much to take in, let alone deal with. I, for one, had a hard time wrapping my head around the fact that someone could love me so much, without condition or reservation—especially after knowing all of the unlovable things I've done. To me, it seemed impossible . . . make-believe . . . fake. And because I struggled with this one truth, I made the choice not to trust God. I pushed Him away, focused on other things, and lived a life separate from Him.

Besides, haven't we all heard it before?

Whether it's the evangelicals that show up at your front door asking if you've found God, or the parishioners walking into worship

> *Don't let anyone talk you out of what God's trying to talk you into.*
> **—Unknown**

each Sunday as you drive by on your way to the mall—rather than choosing to seek our heavenly Father—many of us (me included) have made excuses instead. We've justified our reasons why we were unable to make it to church last week—or any week for that matter. We've told ourselves that God's not worth our time. We've pardoned our lack of attention, focus, and devotion toward our Creator with lame excuses. One after another.

But why? Why do we make these justifications when that craving, that hunger, that longing is present, welling up in our chests, waiting to be fed? Why do we put other things in front of Him time and time again?

> Do not conform to the pattern of this world, but be transformed by the renewing of your mind. Then you will be able to test and approve what God's will is— his good, pleasing and perfect will.
> —Romans 12:2

I don't have an answer, nor do I understand why I've been found guilty of the exact same thing. I don't know why I looked at God as an inconvenience in my life rather than the One who is my life. I'm not sure why I made the world around me my foundation, and what I held most sacred. But I did.

I get it. It's easy to make excuses. It seems way more convenient to spend our Sundays sleeping in, relaxing, and enjoying some much-needed rest as opposed to a sermon at church. It appears easier to live our lives in the hustle and bustle than to seek some quiet time with God. But you know what I've realized? Life without my Savior is pretty empty, kind of pointless, and just plain hard. And the thing about those excuses we keep conjuring up is that eventually . . . they run out.

So, tell me: When it comes to the practice of faith, what's really holding you back from a relationship with God? Are your doubts taking over? Is fear consuming your thoughts? I understand. Remember, I've struggled with all of this myself. And I'd be lying if I told you that there aren't moments when I still wrestle with some of these issues today. So, if you're feeling stuck, wondering if God's always with you like He promises—and in an effort to experience authentic faith—we've got to rid ourselves of those excuses. That's right. We've got to clear our minds from that old way of thinking.

Because it's time for a fresh start—a do-over. It's time to push that reset button on our lives. Now's the time for those doubts to no longer maintain control over our minds.

Doubts and Such

Doubts? Yuck. I hate this word. Even worse, I hate the feeling I get when those uncertainties creep in and loiter about. But we all have them. In fact, you'd be pretty hard-pressed to find a member in the

> *Blessed are those who have not seen and yet have believed.*
> —**John 20:29b**

church today who hasn't had reservations about God at one time or another. Yes. You heard me right. You don't think you're the *only* one who has issues with this, do you? Because how could God (in all of His supreme being) really give a hoot about *us*? And why would He ever long for a relationship with the flawed sinners each of us continually choose to be?

How could He ever love me?

That's the question that popped into my head each and every time I thought about my relationship (or lack thereof) with the Lord. Not only did I doubt His love for me and the importance of having God in my life, but I was ghastly afraid of what it would look like once I *did* let Him in. I was scrambling, clawing, and fighting to stay in this world around me because it was easier to have doubts than to pursue a life of morality and rules. It was easier to remain skeptical than to confront the past (guilt and shame included) I'd have to deal with if I wanted to have a *real* connection with Him.

I simply didn't want to change.

But one of the amazing things about our living God's desires for us (His children) isn't to walk in shame; instead, He wants us to walk in faith (Matt. 21:21). Ultimately, it's okay to have doubts. The more questions one has about our Creator, the better. It means we're yearning for more. It is in our search for Him that a relationship will be established, and a bond will be formed. It's where our journey of faith begins.

> *Teach me your way, LORD, that I may rely on your faithfulness; give me an undivided heart, that I may fear your name.*
> **—Psalm 86:11**

Can I ask you a question? A favor of sorts? What if, just for a little while (or at least for the duration of this book), you let that guard of yours down? And what if (I'm saying "if" here), you allow the wall that so many of us have built up around our hearts to crumble? What if you could vow to trust a little bit more, wipe your mind free from reservation, let God in, and just *believe*?

What do you think might happen?

Let's spend the rest of our time together leading with our hearts while opening our eyes—and our minds—to Him. Because

> *Faith is not something you fall back on; faith is something you step into.*
> **—Liz Curtis Higgs**

this connection you seek to have with God is the one relationship that vows to never let you down.

No matter what you go through, what you do battle against, or how impossible living this life seems to be at times, He's there. No matter how often this faith of ours is going to be tested (and it will be tested), God is sovereign, trustworthy, and all-knowing. Know what else? His promises are guaranteed.

Testing, Testing

You might have been through an awful lot in your life thus far—and the first thing I want to say to you who may be slightly apprehensive at this point, and grappling with issues of trust, is this: you are not alone. So many of us have fallen victim to tragedy, heartache, and

> *Sometimes we stand to learn the most about God from the situations we understand the least.*
> **—Beth Moore**

circumstances that exceed our comprehension. Things that never should have happened have. And these times of great turmoil lead us to question God, His motives, and the reason behind such immense suffering. Moments when we've blamed Him for our troubles, become enraged by our situations, and even sworn Him off due to situations that have transpired in our lives.

Hey, if God *truly* loved us, He wouldn't allow us to go through so much pain, would He? He wouldn't let horrible things happen to *His* children, right? He wouldn't stand by and watch us suffer, stricken with grief and crippled with pain. How could He? You don't do that to someone you love. But it doesn't work this way, friends. Life wasn't set up to be a comfortable ride, free from conflict and void of suffering. Bad things happen, but great things can transpire out of those ashes—out of our despair—if we have faith . . . if we learn to trust in God. Yes—even through the very worst of circumstances.

> *God can use a painful breach of trust in marriage, the heartbreak of an ill child, or a financial blow to bring us back to the basics and remind us how much we need Jesus. The hard seasons make us stronger. Struggling is part of moving forward.*
> **—Kristen Welch**

Know what else? God hurts right along with us. He loves us beyond measure. He's there for us through the worst of our trials and in the midst of our anguish. Our God is in the business of redeeming sorrow for joy.

It's true.

In fact, the Bible holds a number of testimonies filled with accounts of pain, death, misfortune, and yes, misery. But God never abandoned our ancestors in their times of need. He was there all along, carrying them through. And the same is true today. Times may have changed, but God has not.

So, when bad things happen in life—when there seem to be no answers for why they should occur—my mind can't help but wander to Job (pronounced /jōb/). If you're not familiar with this biblical figure, Job was one of the wisest men I've had the pleasure of reading about . . . because his wisdom came from the faith he exhibited during the hardest season of his life. To me, it's one of the most compelling accounts regarding a person's faith, because of the fact that no matter what Satan did to this man, no matter what he took away from him, Job remained faithful to God. He put his trust in the Lord, despite the anger, pain, and frustration he felt. He offered praise in the midst of great suffering. Job remained loyal to God even though Satan had attacked his family and stripped him of all his worldly possessions. He fully believed that his heavenly Father would, sustain him . . . that He would watch over and protect him (Job

> *Through the good. Through the not-so-good. And even through the down right awful—we will trust God. Now this doesn't mean we won't cry and express hurt. But it does mean we've decided it's better to have lived trying to take leaps of faith with God, than to walk away from Him.*
> —**Lysa Terkeurst**

10:12). And ultimately, that's exactly what happened—God rewarded Job for being His dutiful, faithful, and devoted servant and Satan was defeated.

Ladies, I've gotta tell you—our faith is bound to be tested throughout our lives. It's a given. And rather than be surprised when those times come—when those trials present themselves— we're better off knowing they're to be expected. This life wasn't meant to be easy. Sometimes it's going to be unfair, unjust, and even downright cruel. I don't really have to tell you this, because none of us are strangers to heartache at this point, are we? We each have a story, and the scars to remind us of the battles we've fought—the struggles we've endured.

I've had my fair share, too.

"Something may be wrong"—the four words in the English language no parent wants to hear. Ever. The same words we fear from the moment our children enter our world . . . and I had just heard them. Only two months after becoming a regular churchgoer, on the road to getting my faith and marriage in check, a routine doctor's visit for my eldest child turned into the beginning of my worst nightmare. In an instant, my life changed; my heart sunk, and my newfound faith was on trial like never before.

Over the next couple of months, my family found ourselves visiting numerous specialists, enduring rounds of testing—fearing the worst. We heard terminology such as "genetic disorder," "life-threatening," and "spontanous death." To be honest, it felt as though I was in some type of bad dream, or a scene from a movie that I would typically waste a whole box of tissues on . . . but this drama had just become my reality. This was playing out in real life. With *my* daughter . . . *my* baby.

But here's where my *faith* came into play.

From the very moment our doctor speculated at a diagnosis and throughout the twelve agonizing weeks of waiting my husband and I endured in order to receive our daughter's test results, God *never* left me. Even though my faith was new and Satan was attacking, God held my family ever so near. In fact, I drew closer to Him, I prayed every chance I could for His will to match my own, and my faith in my Father became stronger than I ever could have imagined. As the woman who once chose to push God away, I was now relying on the Lord to see me through.

And His presence meant everything.

After a long period of waiting (in what felt like an eternity), we finally received the news we had prayed, hoped, and pleaded for—my daughter's test results came back negative. *Negative*. The doctors were baffled, we were elated, and God had provided us with a miracle. He told me to trust Him, He asked for me to believe in Him, and He begged me to know Him . . . and then He presented me with a miracle.

Now, this isn't to say that a happy ending always occurs in a major life event like ours. But throughout each ordeal we face, we must trust in the Lord. God *knows* what He's doing. His abiding love is constant; His plan, sovereign. We need to rely on our faith, believe His Word, and place our trust—our lives—in the Lord's hands. We must learn to release our issues with control and let God be God.

> *When life doesn't make sense, an explanation*
> *doesn't ease your pain; the presence of God does.*
> **—Rick Warren**

The Gift of Faith

We've already established the fact that somewhere along the way—somewhere in this great big adventure of life, many of us have lost our way—our faith. Or maybe we're completely unaware of just how much we need God, the presence of the Holy Spirit, and Jesus Christ.

> *Trust in the LORD with all your heart, and lean not on your own understanding; in all your ways acknowledge Him, and He shall direct your paths.*
> **—Proverbs 3:5–6 NKJV**

Throughout this book, my plan is to provide you with the opportunity to hear from others besides me: sisters in Christ who carry amazing testimonies, women who have dedicated their lives and ministries to discipling others on behalf of Jesus—all with stories to share. Their experiences are real, heartfelt, and written with you in mind because we've all been in the same spot you are right now. Each one of us has battled the Enemy, and each one of us has struggled in our walk. However, we've discovered the reward and the victory that comes from a journey with Jesus, and we've realized the only way to get through this life is to rely on Him, trust in His Word, and dedicate our lives for His glory.

> *Faith is the measure to which we believe God is God. And faith is the measure to which we let God be God.*
> **—Jennie Allen**

Friend, here is the first of those testimonies . . .

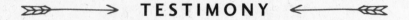

TESTIMONY

The Gift of a Smile
Tracy Steel

My mother adored sending greeting cards to everyone she loved. She affectionately finished every card with her name and her signature smiley face. But it didn't end there. My mom had yellow smiley-face pencils . . . and even coffee mugs. In fact, the walls of her second-grade classroom were adorned with all kinds of these happy, little yellow faces, too. So, it was only appropriate that I was able to find (and wear) the perfect yellow dress on the day we gathered to remember and celebrate her life.

In the spring of 2001, my mother was diagnosed with breast cancer. It was a lengthy illness and arduous battle; on August 24, 2012, she made the difficult decision to end her chemotherapy treatments. And just like that, the doctors immediately placed her in hospice, while I boarded a plane and flew home to be with her and the rest of my family.

But prior to getting that phone call, I received a gift in the mail. As I unwrapped the package, I saw a pair of bright-yellow flip-flops . . . and sat there stunned: they just happened to match the dress I planned to wear at my mother's "Celebration of Life."

And as I tried them on, I couldn't help but chuckle as the tears began to fall. It was not by coincidence that a woman—someone I hadn't talked to in a while—just happened to be strolling down a shoe aisle, and just happened to see this particular pair of bright-yellow flip-flops that she felt the need to surprise me with.

"Just happened" doesn't occur where faith is concerned. Faith replaces "just happened" with "what is." Faith opened my eyes to the excellence, care, and comfort of God that day in a way I hadn't been shown before.

On October 8, 2012, I was by my mother's side when God ushered her into heaven. Later that day, I cut the price tag off of those yellow flip-flops I'd been blessed with. It was time to wear them. As I gathered with family and friends to celebrate my mother's life, I wore my yellow dress and my bright yellow shoes adorned with my favorite bows. I couldn't help but smile as my faith reassured me of another "what is" that day—my mama was home, healed, and happy.

As I write this, the first anniversary of her death is approaching. Whenever I wear my yellow bow-adorned flip-flops, I am reminded of the God-given gift of faith. Faith that serves as a constant reminder . . . faith that helps me to see God's unconditional love for me and His involvement in my life. It gives me the strength to celebrate when common sense beckons me to despair.

Over the past year, many have wondered if the pain associated with my mother's death has caused me to question my faith. There's no denying I've endured a lot of sadness, but rather than question why, her passing has made me sure of my faith! I no longer doubt who God is, even though I sometimes wrestle with all that He allows to happen. This isn't necessarily a bad thing I guess—just a reminder that we're human. God created me . . . and you, too. His patience, mercy, and love toward us are unending.

My faith is not built on circumstances or emotion. It is based and built on Jesus Christ alone. The Bible helps me to understand who He is. The precious truths it contains are what I cling to, what I repeat over and over as I walk through seasons of grief. Having faith doesn't exempt me from heartache either. Rather, faith gives me purpose—it helps me to experience pleasure in the midst of my pain.

When I find myself doubting, I remember my yellow flip-flops with the bows. I remember how Jesus died on the cross so my mother's life would not be lost. I recall the countless ways God protects and provides for me. I pray and ask God for more faith. I look for answers, encouragement, and hope in the Bible. I continue to wait on and trust in God because of who He is.

Faith, like a bow, encircles my weary, broken, and scattered heart. Faith is a gift most precious . . . to me and to God. It's everything.

Prescription for Praise

READ:

Heaven is for Real by Todd Burpo
The Case for Christ by Lee Strobel
The Case for Faith by Lee Strobel
God, I'm Ready to Walk in Faith by Thelma Wells
What Happens When Women Walk in Faith by Lysa TerKeurst
Crazy Love by Francis Chan
The Purpose-Driven Life by Rick Warren
Fed Up with Flat Faith by Kathy Howard
Unshakeable Faith by Kathy Howard
Aha by Kyle Idleman

STUDY:

Hebrews 11:1
1 John 5:4
Hebrews 11:6
Ephesians 2:8–9
2 Corinthians 5:6–7
Ephesians 6:16
Matthew 21:21–22
1 Peter 2:6
Romans 8:18

SING:

"What Faith Can Do," performed by Kutless
"Steady My Heart," performed by Kari Jobe
"How Great is Our God" performed by Matthew Sgherzi

"Lead Me to the Cross," performed by Hillsong
"Indescribable," performed by Chris Tomlin
"Times," performed by Tenth Avenue North
"You Revive Me," performed by Christy Nockels

APPLY:

1. Where do you struggle most when it comes to your faith?

_____

_____

2. Do you have doubts about God in general? If so, list them here.

_____

_____

3. What's preventing you from casting your doubts aside? Why do you think you're holding on to them?

_____

_____

4. Explain what it is that led you to pick up this book and want to read it. What are you hoping to find? Change?

_____

_____

5. What do you think this verse means as it applies to one's faith: Matthew 14:29–31?

_____

_____

God created us to walk with Him, to know Him, and to be loved by Him. He is our living well, and when we drink from the water, He continually provides. His living water will change us.

—**Courtney Joseph,** *Women Living Well*

Note:
1   Kathy Howard, "One Fun Size M&Ms Leads to Another," *Unshakeable Faith for Life* (blog), November 1, 2012, http://www.kathyhoward.org/one-fun-size-mms-leads-to-another/.

CHAPTER 2

Amazing Grace

Amazing grace! How sweet the sound
that saved a wretch like me!
I once was lost, but now I'm found;
was blind, but now I see.

—John Newton

Chances are you've heard this song before. Most of us have. But have you ever really studied its words? Have you ever broken down the content of this hymn and actually thought about the meaning behind these simple yet powerful lyrics?

Up until my reunion with Christ a little less than a decade ago, I never really paid much attention to it either. The numerous times I did hear it, I considered the song to be pleasant, sort of catchy, and even found myself humming along to its tune on occasion—but I never thought about the significance *behind* it, nor the depth of what this piece was trying to say.

I just didn't get it.

Today it's a much different story. When I hear "Amazing Grace," I'm brought to tears by its message. Every. Single. Time. And the reason is simple. After accepting Jesus into my heart, ridding myself of shame, and embracing the grace He so willingly offers, I finally understand and am well aware of the pardon granted to me . . . the grace I've been given—*we've* been given! Keep in mind, it's nothing we've earned nor is it something we can buy, beg, or barter for either. Instead it's been afforded to us by God, through His Son's sacrifice.

> *All have sinned and are falling short of the honor* and *glory which God bestows and receives.*
> **—Romans 3:23** AMP

And let me tell you—it's deep. It's heavy. It's unbelievably emotional. It's so liberating to know that my yucky old sins have been forgiven.

It's freeing to realize that these days I'm no longer blind to what's been sacrificed for me.

Now I *see*.

I'm no longer that lost girl trying to work her way through life by controlling her circumstances. Instead, I'm *found* in (and through) Christ.

> *God's love cannot be explained, only experienced.*
> **—Staypositive.me**

I'm no longer considered a wretch consumed by her sins.

Because I've been *saved*.

Oh, and this salvation I speak of is nothing short of amazing.

It's nothing short of a miracle.

Sweet Salvation

*Since God forgets the sins you've confessed to him,
why do you keep reminding yourself?*
—Rick Warren

Right now, you might be scratching your head, pondering the concept of this whole salvation thing and asking yourself *What does it mean to be saved?* How does one define grace and then wrap their brain around the fact that it's ours (pro bono) and up for the taking? Nothing is free these days, right? But it appears the biggest—and best—gift any of us could ever receive is, in fact, free. The price has already been paid.

Yep—forgiveness of sins, grace, and eternal salvation are all up for grabs if we make the decision to accept Christ . . . to follow His lead and profess Him as our Lord and Savior. Girls, if we could just step back for a moment, stop hesitating, and invite the Lord into our hearts, we'd realize the endless possibilities that await us thanks to the

> *For it is by grace you
> have been saved,
> through faith—and this
> is not from yourselves,
> it is the gift of God—
> not by works, so that
> no one can boast.*
> **—Ephesians 2:8–9**

actions of Jesus Christ. We would be awestruck and amazed. We would be forever changed because this type of love, and the eternal promise it guarantees—this grace that blankets our sins—is an absolute game changer.

But why would God care so much? Why would a guy like Jesus go to such lengths—to allow Himself to be tortured, ridiculed, spat on, and crucified(!) in order to save you and me from our sins? Who would willingly do something like that?

The sort of affection our heavenly Father's dishing out isn't your typical kind of love, now is it? It's kinda crazy in fact. I mean, for God to sacrifice His Son (and a form of Himself) for billions who have all fallen short of His glory (Rom. 3:23, 5:7)—you and I both know that we just don't see that type of devotion anywhere. Suffering is the atoning work of Jesus, and it's why this message I'm sharing with you is so special—and why this book you're reading is necessary. Our God is amazing, one of a kind, all powerful, and almighty. The grace He bestows is incomparable just as the eternal life we'll inherit is undeniable.

Jesus is Lord.

And if we say it, we're just a strain of words. But if we say it, and believe it deep in our hearts and with every fiber of our God-given being, we will be saved. If we speak it with our tongues, we will be spared (Rom. 10:9–10). If we just open our eyes, clear our minds, and prepare our hearts, heaven will be ours . . . and it'll be much, much more than any of us can possibly imagine.

But I know you, friend—as you sit there, reading these words, full of questions—I sense your skepticism, your resistance. *Is it really free? Could the whole idea of grace and salvation be so easy to attain? Or like everything else in this life, are there strings attached?*

Growing up, my thoughts on salvation came with some pretty mixed reviews. As far as I was concerned, I kinda owed Jesus a whole heck of a lot for going to that cross for me. It felt as though I was being placed on a major guilt trip from the moment I stepped foot into the church sanctuary. On those rare occasions when I did attend worship services, I must confess that the last thing I wanted to do was make eye contact with the ginormous version of Jesus, hanging on a cross in front of me. It was all I could do to keep my focus off of Him as I tried to look away, look down, and everywhere else except to fixate on the replica of my Savior—His side gashed open, the rags surrounding His waist, bloodied, those large nails holding His fate in place, and that horrible crown of thorns piercing His skull.

The guilt was overwhelming as I was forced to confront that image, that symbol . . . that cross. I felt unworthy, ashamed even, in those moments . . . and for a young kid, it was all a little too much to bear.

As if that wasn't bad enough, my peripheral vision couldn't help but register the "stations" surrounding me: up on those church walls, fourteen scenes depicting Christ's journey to the cross were on display, begging for me to turn and glance. *Look and see what this man, your Christ, your God, has done for you,* they commanded, as I sat there, breathing in the guilt, all the while estranging myself from my Creator. There was Jesus, beaten, unable to go on any longer. There was Mary, His mother, weeping at His feet. And there I was, weighed down by the overwhelming pressure I felt as I thought about the true cost of my salvation. So rather than embrace this gift—this "freebie," His grace and mercy—I used it as a means to distance myself instead.

I couldn't disappoint God if I didn't know Him.

Besides, the last thing I wanted to do was upset Him with my sinner's ways. Nor did I particularly care to be slapped on the hand, reprimanded, or made to feel worse than I already did due to my choices either. I wanted to love God, just as I wanted to embrace Jesus—but I didn't know how. I felt so undeserving . . . I felt so alone.

The whole idea of grace and unconditional love was totally lost on my fourteen-year-old self. I couldn't see past my shame in order to experience His love. And no one was telling me otherwise. But those discouraging thoughts and episodes of guilt don't hold me captive like they used to. Instead, those two wood planks represent my freedom, liberty, and salvation—that cross is a symbol of absolute love. There's no guilt when I look at it these days—only appreciation, understanding, and immense gratitude.

> *Our salvation is really about so much more than just us. God*
> *lovingly redeems us through the blood of His precious Son,*
> *and displays perfect patience as He transforms us from sinners*
> *to saints. Not just so that we can have all the benefits of*
> *walking with Him, but also so that those around us—*
> *those who are watching, and will one day bow their knee to*
> *Him as Lord—can have His work in us as an example of what*
> *He can also do for them. (based on 1 Tim. 1:12–16)*
> **—Brooke McGlothlin**

As for the young girl sitting in that church pew so long ago, eyes cast downward, hands folded, filled with fear, unaware of what her salvation really meant—I'd give her the same advice I'm about to share with you: *that* Man on *that* cross loves you more than anything . . . anything! And all He's asking in return is for you and me to give Him our hearts, to trust in and rely on Him throughout this life. Know this: what He went through wasn't to cause you guilt or shame. It was done in love. God's love for you is eternal. He made you, He knit you in the womb (Ps. 139:13), He's always there for you, and His plans for your life far exceed your own expectations (Jer. 29:11). This is why He sacrificed His Son—Himself! So, follow Him. Apply His teachings. Immerse yourself in the Bible and realize that those trespasses you're bound to do battle with—He'll extend mercy. Those temptations

> *He will cover you*
> *with his feathers, and*
> *under his wings you*
> *will find refuge.*
> **—Psalm 91:4**

you might be fooled into believing—He's there, waiting to shed some much-needed grace upon you.

God. Is. For. You. No exceptions—He loves us all, and the eternal life He promises is for real. Embrace it, friend.

Breaking Bad

He who began a good work in you will
carry it on to completion until the day of Jesus Christ.
—Philippians 1:6

We all have our own story. Indeed, every single one of us was created with a unique blueprint—and we lead very different lives. Up until this point, you may have led a life you're not overly ecstatic about, nor particularly proud of. There may have been instances and events you wish you could forget, behaviors you're too embarrassed to admit, actions you want to rescind, and seasons you wish you could change.

And for each one of you who is reading these words, and nodding your head in agreement, please know that there are countless others doing the same. For those who are struggling at this very moment, wallowing in guilt, and paralyzed by shame, this is what you must know: God chose you from the beginning.

Did you breathe that in?

Despite what your current situation may be or how far your path has veered, you have a purpose, a plan, and a role in His kingdom. Even through your toughest trials, your story's taking place, unfolding, being revealed. Your testimony's being written . . . and possibly rewritten.

And you're not alone.

By the time I finally raised my white flag to Christ, my marriage was in serious trouble. My world was closing in around me, crashing down—busting at the seams. I was losing at this game of life (big-time), because I was allowing something else—make that someone else—to pull the strings. And judging from my decisions at the time, it wasn't God. I was willingly permitting the Enemy to take up residence within, and he was doing some serious damage in the process.

However, God can take those poor decisions we've made, and the horrible habits we've found our way into, and He can turn them around. He can take all of that bad, and break it for good. But we've got to be open to it, girls, ready for change—willing to accept. And we've got to be genuine in our efforts.

You see, I ignored His voice, discounted His Word, and reneged on a relationship with God for way too long. I abused His grace— used it as something I could fall back on when the urge struck me—not realizing that the gifts of grace and mercy are not to be taken lightly. In fact, nothing that God has provided should be taken for granted and my own embarassment emerged when I realized that's exactly what I'd done. I was ashamed of those moments in my life when I heard His call and willfully chose to disobey, when I knew right from wrong but made poor decisions anyway.

Can you relate? Have there been times when you've known it was God tugging at your heart, but discounted that pull in an effort to hold on to free will, to have control, to do what you wanted rather than what He desired for your life? It's so easy to take that path, isn't it?

But God sees us—the real us. He knows our weaknesses. He's familiar with our demons . . . and He understands our struggles.

God is there for you no matter what. In His eyes, there are no losers or lost souls—there's no name-calling or labeling either.

Broken or whole. You. Are. His.

Do you get that? I mean *really* get it? No matter what this world tells you, no matter how much you hurt or how scarred you've become, your heavenly Father loves and wants you. He's able to take away that sin, by redeeming the sinner. We just have to accept it. And we need to live as He's called us to . . . by His rules, His way.

God is stronger than every broken thing within me.
—**Angela Thomas**

TESTIMONY

The Battle is Real
Heather S. Riggleman

Tears streamed down my face from fear and the humiliation of being hand-cuffed as police officers hauled me through the emergency room doors. The cocktail of drugs and alcohol were already reacting dangerously; my heart started beating wildly and I began to lose consciousness. Minutes felt like hours. In fact, it took four police officers to hold me down while a doctor and team of nurses attempted to pump my stomach and hold my mouth open in an effort to make me ingest activated charcoal. And that's when I heard the audible voice of God: *"Heather, I have plans for you; you are not done yet."*

Stunned, I lay back in silence as an overwhelming presence of peace filled the room.

You see, I'm the girl with a past. I'm the girl at your church, office, or PTA meeting with a whole history behind her. Not just a few silly mistakes in college either. More like the girl with scars from past abuse, addictions, and other self-inflicted wounds. I'm the girl who avoids eye contact with cops, bartenders, old friends, and counselors. And rather than coming to grips with the girl I used to be, I put on my mask instead and hide behind the woman I've become, one who's since exhibited responsibility, strength, and poise. One who thought she needed to prove her self-worth and appreciation for God's grace by her own strength . . . by her own will.

When I initially accepted Jesus Christ as my Savior, it felt so good to know that my sketchy past and arrest records had been washed clean. But it wasn't enough. I continued to hide behind that mask; I became responsible—to look good by society's standards, I made sure my kids were well behaved, and that my home was spotless. I "owned" this sort of responsibility when the painful events occurred, too. When I miscarried I thought it was because I wasn't taking care of myself or maybe it was God's way of telling me I shouldn't have any more children—talk about warped thinking! When bad things happened, I assumed it was my fault. Instead of allowing Jesus to be liable for me, I owned my sins . . . I owned my mistakes. In other words, I was attempting to be Jesus, to maintain control . . . and it wasn't working.

Not at all.

It wasn't until I broke down in front of my church ministry team that I finally understood what grace was all about. After a particularly not-so-pleasant staff meeting, I got up and left, as in, walked out (!) . . . and guess who was the one in charge! But later that afternoon, as I sipped my coffee and looked out the window, I sifted through memories—trying to figure out if I was truly forgiven. And that's when I heard God whisper, *"You may have accepted my Son, but you didn't accept my gift of grace."*

I was stunned; tears fell from my eyes.

Girls, God isn't some cranky old man upstairs who's bored and meddlesome, nor is He ready to strike us dead the instant we say a curse word for dropping the jar of sugar on the floor. God saw me as His little girl trying to save the world, something I could never do since it took all of His love to do it through Jesus. Jesus is grace. Grace is God showing His love for us even though we don't deserve it. You can't earn God's grace just as you don't deserve to be saved from your mistakes, but God bestows it upon us, rescuing us from sin's punishment.

Grace means God doesn't focus on your failures, your shortcomings, or your darkest secrets—instead, He sees His girl in need of a Savior. Grace gives us the strength we need to make it through, it lets us trust in and hold on to the things God has promised. Grace is a luminous string of pearls, representing each of your todays and tomorrows—knowing that whatever happens, God has given you the gift to be free of sin. Grace is the journey to freedom and the knowledge that He's waiting for you at the end of the road.

You need to release the load that God never meant you to carry, and focus on what He has called you to do.
—Kahlia Cathcart

Get It and Give It

The more aware we are of our need for God's grace, the more generous we will be towards others.
—Richard Blackaby, *Putting a Face on Grace*

Here's a newsflash: grace (and the act thereof) isn't solely meant for us to obtain. Thus far, we've chatted about what it means to receive grace, but we have yet to explore what dishing out a huge helping of this stuff toward another looks like. After all, "grace" is an action, and a practice we need to display. It's living out God's example of how we should treat one another. You know, as a mother, wife, Christian, and human being, I have the opportunity to extend grace multiple times a day. Sadly, most of the time, I find myself doing the opposite. Like when my toddler writes on the television with permanent marker, or when the lady in front of me at the ATM is taking her sweet time trying to get cash. Day after day, moments arise where we have the choice to elect grace over anger, but how often do we opt for the latter instead of the former? How many times do we resort to frustration instead of exhibiting kindness? When I think of the grace I receive from God (thanks to Jesus), I can't believe how often I refuse to bestow the same upon another.

So how do we do it?

In offering grace, we're letting go of our need for control. We're intentionally taking the necessary steps to ensure someone is excused for their behavior—even if they don't necessarily deserve it. See, grace is a gift we receive but it is also one we can impart. To the child who didn't understand that the television set wasn't his blank canvas, I can extend grace for his actions. For the woman who is completely unaware of the rush I am in and lacks any type of consideration (or ATM etiquette), I can offer a full pardon as well.

If we're more than willing to accept grace from God, then we ought to be ready to grant some of it in return.

But what does this look like?

Well, it looks the same way it does when Jesus gives grace to us. It's unmerited favor. There's no guilt or shame. You don't forget what happened either; you just choose to replace harsh words and even consequences with an act of love instead. You make the choice not to react negatively. Whether or not others are genuinely sorry for their trespasses, we can choose to forgive them. Indeed, we *can* extend grace.

Is it easy? Not really.

It's pretty hard at times to bite that tongue, isn't it? Especially when the sitcom you're watching can no longer be seen correctly due to the drawn-in mustaches all over your television screen. Or when you end up being five minutes late to a job interview because of the woman who took too long trying to decide how much cash she should remove from the ATM.

But God gives us grace over and over again. We mess up, we get grace. This stuff abounds! However, we need to understand that the gift of grace cost Christ His life. So, if we can continually accept pardons for our own transgressions, then shouldn't we provide the same gift to others in our lives?

In comparison, maybe the ATM issues and problems with the television aren't such a big deal after all. And maybe the idea of grace should be kept in mind when wrongdoings occur against us . . . when anger wells up inside.

Getting grace is amazing. But giving it and honoring God in the process? Even better.

> *My chains are gone. I've been set free.*
> *My God, my Savior has ransomed me.*
> **—Chris Tomlin, "Amazing Grace"**

Prescription for Praise

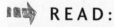 **READ:**

One Thousand Gifts by Ann Voskamp
Grace for the Good Girl by Emily P. Freeman
Grace by Max Lucado
Grace Happens Here by Max Lucado
What's So Amazing about Grace? by Philip Yancey
Follow Me by David Platt

STUDY:

Ephesians 2:8
Ephesians 1:7
Romans 3:24

Romans 12:6
2 Corinthians 9:14
2 Timothy 1:9
2 Peter 3:18
Hebrews 13:9
1 Corinthians 15:10
John 1:17

 # SING:

"Amazing Grace" performed by Chris Tomlin
"Your Grace Is Enough" performed by Matt Maher
"Grace" performed by Michael W. Smith
"Redeemed" performed by Big Daddy Weave
"Grace Like Rain" performed by Todd Agnew

APPLY:

1. As we learned, grace has been afforded to us for free. How does this make you feel and are you able to grasp the meaning of such a gift? Explain.

_____

_____

2. After reading Ephesians 2:8–9, jot down your thoughts. What are these verses saying to you about your own life? Your salvation?

_____

_____

3. How does receiving God's grace change your perception of yourself?

_____

_____

4. Why do we need grace, and how do you plan to extend grace to others?

_____

_____

5. Using your computer's search engine, find and listen to the hymn "Amazing Grace." What do you think? Like me, do you understand the meaning behind these lyrics a bit better? Explain.

_____

_____

[The Lord] said to me, "My grace is sufficient for you,
for my power is made perfect in weakness." Therefore
I will boast all the more gladly about my weaknesses,
so that Christ's power may rest on me.
—2 Corinthians 12:9

CHAPTER 3

Forgiveness: Unconditional Love

When we forgive, we leave anger to find joy. We leave hatred to find love. We leave dysfunction to find stability. We leave judgment to find compassion.

—Suzanne Eller

Regrets. Mistakes. Sins.

Well this sounds like a fun chapter, now doesn't it (enter sarcasm)?

Chances are though, if you're human, you've had to confront these three bad boys at some point in your life. Maybe you've made some poor choices in the past, resulting in personal regrets. Or maybe you're a woman who's been wounded in such a way that the bitterness (the kind you can't help but hold on to) is restricting your ability to move forward, on with your life, and past the pain.

This whole "mercy" thing is incredibly hard to do, and whether you're attempting to pardon yourself or another, sometimes—okay, make that *most* of the time—forgiveness can seem downright impossible.

But forgiveness is about repenting for our sins, accepting our imperfections, and giving ourselves some grace. It's recognizing that the type of love Christ is handing out is absolute. Total. Complete. It's understanding that if the Man who went to the cross for my sins can still love me after everything *I've* done, then I guess I should be able to award myself (as well as another) with the same type of gift . . . the same type of grace.

Easier said than done though.

Let's face it: we've all slipped up (Rom. 3:23). We're all guilty (yuck, there's that word) of doing something we're not proud of. Whether it's hurting another with our words and/or actions, or messing up in a way that the world around us could never pardon, we *all* have sinned. And those mistakes we've made frequently flood our minds with regret as we're left pondering the error of our ways—like a CD on repeat function we can't help from playing said events over and over again in our minds. We can't break free. Indeed, it's those lapses in good judgment (and the remorse that accompanies them) that tend to hold us captive—as we find ourselves in trouble with a friend, a spouse, a loved one, or even the law.

And if this is you, well, you've got company, my friend. Because it was me, too.

June 2007 (Journal entry)

It's a decision I can never take back.

And it's left me questioning my entire being. I've hated who I've become, and often erupt into anger over the stupidity of my actions. I cry often, laugh little, and constantly think about the mistakes I've made. The way I've hurt my loved ones, damaged a relationship, and broken a trust. These choices can't be undone no matter how hard I try, or how badly I want to.

It's as if I spend more time focused on the sin that was committed rather than the forgiveness I've been extended, and there's a reason: I see the disappointment in their faces, the hurt in their eyes, and I know I'm the cause of it.

I'm the reason they're struggling and the forgiveness I desire above all else seems impossible to receive.

Except for One.

This guy, Jesus—He went to battle in order to wipe these sins of mine away. Pure as snow, washed clean. I'm forgiven by Him. I am loved.

In His eyes, I am redeemed.

And I guess that's all that should matter.

But I'm still struggling. I'm sickened by who and what I see in the mirror. I've turned into the girl I never thought I'd be.

Gosh, I've spent years (years!) beating myself up over the lousy decisions I've made, wishing them away—incapable of fully grasping the magnitude of God's grace. It's a horrible space to live in, and so here's what I have to say to you who might be doing the same thing: He loves you without reservation, and minus all those "buts" and "what ifs." He may not like the way you're living or the sin that's taken place, but He loves you in spite of it all.

God may hate sin, but He could never hate *you*.

So, when it comes to forgiveness, here's what you need to remember: it's waiting for you. Take your negative thoughts, your doubts, your regrets, and all of the guilt and shame you're consistently bombarding yourself with, and place it in God's hands.

Purge that pain and self-hatred and send it straight to Him. Get rid of it. That's what He wants, for you to feel free, for you to breathe again, and for you to see yourself as He sees you. Ask for it, sweet sister, and indeed—you shall receive (Matt. 7:7).

And then?

Never look back.

TESTIMONY

Girl, Don't Look Back—You're Forgiven
Joanne Kraft

Forgiven. One word packs a mighty punch, doesn't it? It holds the power to release even the most painful heartache and redeem what we mistakenly believe we've made irreversible in our lives. Why is it that once I put my hand in God's that I continued to punish myself for past mistakes? Somehow I felt being forgiven wasn't enough. Ultimately, I was telling Jesus His work on the cross was less than perfect to help me.

There are lots of things that can trip me up as I walk along this journey of faith. I'm a spiritual late bloomer. Jesus and I began our love story when I was already a mother of two. (I never said I was the brightest tool in the shed.) Before I met Christ, I apparently liked learning about life the hard way. Oh, what a different world I live in now with Jesus beside me!

Still, there's one way I painfully trip myself up from time to time, one thing that keeps me from knowing I'm forgiven or believing I'm a new creation and that I'm not the same person I was before. For me it's "looking back."

My Polygraph Test

My husband is my reluctant passenger whenever we travel down memory lane. Once I put on my turn signal and head toward Recollection Road his body stiffens and his eyes roll back in his head in silent protest. It is at that very moment that I commit a felony, a marriage felony: I become his kidnapper and he becomes my hostage. Any questions I ask him like, "Paul, do you remember that time . . . ?" or "Paul, have you ever . . . ?" can instantly transform his countenance.

While pursuing a job at a local police department, I took a polygraph test. For the first time in a long while, I was able to understand and even share my husband's pain.

It may not be fair to compare the stress of a polygraph test with looking back or taking a quick trip into the past, but I can't help but feel that the similarities are striking. Like my husband, as soon as the polygraph technician began asking me questions, I immediately tensed up. She asked things like, "As far back as you can remember, have you ever stolen something from your employer . . . even as a teenager?" I silently thought, *As far back as I can remember? Seriously? A teenager? Are we going back that far!?*

My mind was trying to work the numbers to figure out if my infractions were still admissible in court. I was thinking of answers even before the technician asked the questions. I nervously wondered if there is a statute of limitations on stolen peanut butter cups. At one point I almost blurted out loud, "I never inhaled!" As my mind raced I became anxious; should I call an attorney to have legal representation for the remainder of this test? As the questions continued, just like my husband, my eyes began to roll into the back of my head.

It didn't help that I was sitting in this man-made, evil time machine. The chair was monitoring my breathing, my sweat production, and my heart rate. Almost like an electric chair without the electricity. But instead, I was the one who wanted to die. Some of the questions brought back memories that I was not excited to talk about, while other questions brought back memories I was not too proud of and even more that are actually quite shameful.

Don't Look Back

As I drove home from my test I felt miserable. Like any intelligent woman who had just thrown up every bad memory, I began my trek home by drowning my sorrows in a double cheeseburger and triple-thick milkshake. My past was laced with sins that I had not thought of in a long time.

I couldn't help but think of the story in Genesis when the angels grabbed Lot and his wife and daughters by the hand and pulled them to safety from the destruction soon to befall Sodom and Gomorrah. "As soon as they had brought them out, one of [the angels] said, "Flee for your lives! Don't look back, and don't stop anywhere in the plain!" (Gen. 19:17). What a command to this family!

Not only were they to flee for their lives, they were ordered not to look back. They weren't to saunter, stroll, or even loiter in their past. What a command for me, too. The Lord gave this command to protect me from feeling miserable. Well, of course I was feeling miserable. I had just spent three unusually long hours meandering down the road of my sinful past.

God's Word says I am not to look back there and not even to stop anywhere along that road of remembrance. Romans 8:1 popped into my head: "There is now no condemnation for those who are in Christ Jesus." Another verse my girlfriend had just reminded me of the day before came to mind: "He has taken our sins from us as far as the east is from the west" (Ps. 103:12 NLV). And then there was 2 Corinthians 5:17:"Therefore, if anyone *is* in Christ, he *is* a new creation; old things have passed away; behold, all things have become new" (NKJV). It was only after washing my mind in God's Word that I again had peace.

God's peace is a by-product of His gift of grace. Undeserving, unmerited favor is the salve that heals us from the inside out. While dying from cancer, my mother was not aware of this blessed gift. She was a beautiful woman and mother, yet the burden she carried from her past sins was heartbreaking to watch. Six weeks before her death she surrendered her life to the Lord, and only then was she able to sleep peacefully and without fear or tears. She had been held hostage by her past for far too long.

The Enemy of my soul loved every bit of my polygraph test. No doubt he would have loved to keep me back there at my Sodom and Gomorrah days when I lived out my unforgiven life. It was a struggle afterward not to think that this was who I truly am. But, I had learned from a dear friend that whenever I felt myself believing lies, I was to use God's Word as He tells us to, as a sword to slice and dice. Have you ever felt this way? God's Word is supernatural and more powerful than any deep-breathing exercises or eight-hundred-milligram ibuprofen tablet to take away the pain and shame of our past.

Your Past is Past

Here's the truth. My past is past. I am forgiven. God tells me so. He says if I confess my sins, He is faithful and just and will forgive my sins and purify me from all unrighteousness (1 John 1:9). Not only that, but God won't even remember my sins (Heb. 10:17). So why do I?

God has blessed you with an amazing brain. It not only functions as a bad-memory retriever but can bring back to mind many beautiful memories as well. There is nothing wrong with looking back at baby photos of our children or love letters from our husbands. God has gifted us with the ability to look in our life's rearview mirror from time to time to see all of the special moments we have been blessed to have experienced. The reality is that while driving forward we can only look in our rearview mirrors for just a moment. If we were to keep our eyes in that rearview mirror we would not be able to go forward very well and would eventually crash.

Jesus reminds us in the Gospel of Luke, "Remember Lot's wife!" He wants us to be cautious of looking back, because looking back keeps us from moving forward and drawing closer to Him. That is why we call this our "Christian walk", not our "Christian stand" or our "Christian stop." Christianity is a process. As we continue in this supernatural process, we will take steps forward each and every time we grow and mature. Each time we press on toward the prize.

In all uncomfortable moments and trials, I know that, as a child of our King, He promises that He works everything out for good for those who love Him. When you're walking a forgiven path, remember that thoughts which begin as nauseating recollections of the miry muck of your past can become great reminders of God's forgiveness. I am so thankful that I have a Savior and I am redeemed. He has forgiven me and washed me as white as snow.

Each day I make a point to look forward. On this road, with Jesus at the wheel, I will be a willing passenger. And lucky for my husband, I won't be taking any hostages this time.

Good-bye, Good Girl

> *For you are all children of God through faith in Christ Jesus.*
> **—Galatians 3:26** NLT

As I sit here and reflect upon my life thus far, I wish I could say I'd done things differently. I wish I could tell you that I've always lived according to God's Word and will—but I haven't.

No one has.

You see, I've always been the type of girl who's attempted to live her life completely void of mistakes, errors, and regrets. You know—the kind of gal who could look back on her years at the ripe old age of eighty and know with certainty that her time spent on earth was pleasing to others, devoid from any sort of *major* sin, and just plain good. Maybe even perfect.

But who was I kidding?

To think I could exist free from temptation and/or have the power to conquer it without God and His Son in my life? Um, just call me naïve. And consider my ego to be way out of whack in thinking I could do so. I'm just not that strong on my own. I need

God. I need Christ. I need their forgiveness for my transgressions, and the imperfect person I'm continually realizing I am.

I need what they're offering because, as the past has proven, I'm gonna blow it. I've made mistakes in the past and, more than likely, I'm gonna make some again.

Girls, God has blessed us with the power of free will. Each one of us has been provided the opportunity to make decisions all our own. Some are good, but others—maybe not so good. Ever heard of Adam and a gal named Eve? How about the Garden of Eden and the sneaky snake? Free will is a double-edged sword of sorts. It's being able to make those choices—right or wrong—and then deal with the consequences thereof.

Know what else? This whole decision-making process we're at the helm of? It's not always that easy to navigate. We live in a world deeply rooted in temptations. The Enemy is always set to attack, which means if we're not prepared for battle, and if our foundation rests on anything else besides God and His Son, we are bound to fall. Whether we recognize it or not, each one of us walks around with a huge bull's-eye on our backs. We're prime targets . . . sitting ducks for Satan. And lemme tell you, if I've learned anything, it's this: the Enemy is always waiting, always ready . . . and he's a darn good shot.

Living a life in Christ isn't about being perfect, friends; rather, it's about following God's direction . . . His cues. It's about obedience and loyalty. It's living for our living God. Mistakes? They're gonna happen,

> *Forgiveness is the key that unlocks the door of resentment and the handcuffs of hatred.*
> **—Corrie ten Boom**

regrets are bound to occur, and sins are going to transpire. But it's how we respond to and learn from these lapses in judgment that makes all the difference.

Now, I realize some of us are struggling when it comes to brushing off the heaviness that lies on our hearts. Many of us can't. We're in need of moving on, but find ourselves frozen, analyzing our wrongdoings over and over again. We get caught up in thinking about the pain we've caused another, the wrongs that have been committed against us, and the times when we've totally messed up. It's easy to look at the events in our lives and wish them away. It's so simple to feel guilt, shame, and fear for what we've done.

I mean, there's no denying we're flawed, right? But when we fail, when we disobey God, when we screw up royally—forgiveness is ours for the taking. It's there for us to receive.

Perfectionists need not apply.

Forgiving Another?

As if forgiving ourselves isn't hard enough, we're also called to forgive each other (Eph. 4:32). In those instances where we've been wronged—we're expected to forgive the one committing the offense against us.

Ugh.

Forgiving someone else? Most of the time it's the last thing I want to do. No, really. That's not fun to admit but it seems difficult enough just trying to control my emotions, and curb my tongue, let alone shed some grace upon another for the wrong they've sent my way. Whether it's something they said, the way they acted, or how they treated me—let's just say a number of people have trespassed against yours truly. I'm talking ticked me off (as in red hot and slightly fuming), and angered me in such a way that the last thing I'm interested in doing is pardoning their actions.

Ladies, hear me out here: that person who hurt you, pissed you off, or violated you in some way, shape, or form doesn't deserve your forgiveness for what they've done—that's how we feel, right? That's what we're toiling with, amen? But at this moment, you've got to focus on *your* needs, and the freedom *you're* going to receive once you release the burden of being wronged—once you allow Jesus to intervene on your behalf, guide your steps, and help you move through this process. Because it's not about the people that have hurt you, it's about breaking free from the pain—the prison—you've allowed their trespasses to place you in. One where you and you alone hold the key.

Whatever you're dealing with, God is fully aware of the issues weighing heavily on your heart. He sees you. He knows you. Ask for His help in dealing with your hurt, your resentment, your anger, and that bitterness. Allow Him to transform your mind because the hostility and hatred you're holding on to is too much for anyone to bear. Let God remove that burden and work in your heart . . . one breath, one blink, one exhale at a time.

Yes, you need to set those demons free—the ones gnawing at your soul and taking over your mind. Girls—rid yourself from the burden(s) you were never (ever!) meant to carry on your own.

Give it to God.

The Demons Within

We all have them. The voices, I mean. The ones that creep in and fill our minds with doubts and negative feelings. The ones that tell us we're unworthy of grace, undeserving of love, and not worth anyone's time. They're the same voices feeding our anger, persuading us not to trust another, or forgive those who have trespassed against us. They're up there, milling around, infecting our thoughts, and doing damage.

I hate those voices. Not just because of what they tell me but because of the fact that sometimes I actually listen—I believe what they say.

All of the good we learn and know about our God, Satan threatens to destroy. God tells us we're forgiven, just as He tells us to forgive others, but the Enemy fills us with suspicion—causing us to doubt ourselves, His Word, and the promises He's made. I mean, how does one ever truly learn to forgive a person? How are we supposed to get past that sort of hurt—that type of pain? How can God expect us to? How can Jesus ask for something so huge?

In her book *The Unburdened Heart*, Suzanne Eller beautifully depicts what the act of forgiveness should look like, the process one goes through, the battles one faces. In the end, those who can learn to forgive others are ultimately, the ones who find peace. Because forgiveness is about freeing your mind from the hurt, the nega-tivity, and anger your transgressor triggered. It's giving yourself permission to move forward . . . and in turn, setting yourself free.

Forgiveness is freedom.

However, there's not a how-to when it comes to pardoning another. There's not a certain time frame in which to do so either. It's not something that happens quickly or even during the course of reading this book. It's a process. It's difficult. It involves prayer (a lot of it), a ton of soul-searching—and it requires assistance from the Lord.

When you're hurting and when you've been wronged, pray for the strength to forgive, friend. Ask God for the ability to move on . . . give Him the opportunity to free you from your pain. Allow Him to work in and through you. Pray for His presence, and then watch Him get to work.

Prescription for Praise

🎵 READ:

The Mended Heart by Suzanne Eller

The Unburdened Heart by Suzanne Eller

Forgiveness: Breaking the Power of the Past by Kay Arthur, David Lawson, and BJ Lawson

God Loves Broken People by Sheila Walsh

Mended: Pieces of a Life Made Whole by Angie Smith

🎵 STUDY:

Isaiah 43:25

Jeremiah 31:34

Hebrews 8:12

Romans 3:23

Romans 6:23

Psalm 103:12

Colossians 2:14

2 Corinthians 5:17

1 John 1:9

🎵 SING:

"Forgiveness" performed by Matthew West

"Forgiven" performed by Sanctus Real

"East to West" performed by Casting Crowns

"Everything Glorious" performed by the David Crowder Band

"Redeemed" performed by Big Daddy Weave

"Write Your Story" performed by Francesca Battistelli

APPLY:

1. Is there anyone in your life you're currently trying to forgive? Write their name(s) here:

_____

_____

Then pray this prayer:

> *Dear God, I don't know how to forgive this person and honestly, I just don't know if I can—or if I want to. Lord, I am hurt, I am in pain, and You know who's causing it. Give me the strength to forgive because I'm not strong enough to do this on my own. Set me free . . . from the bitterness, hurt, and anger I've been holding on to. Help me, God, to help myself. Free me of this struggle once and for all.*
> *In Jesus' precious name,*
> *Amen!*

2. Why do you think Jesus asks us to forgive others for their trespasses against us? Why would He call us to do something so hard?

_____

_____

3. What would forgiving the person (or persons) you mentioned above mean to you?

_____

_____

4. I want you to think about why you're holding that person (or persons) in contempt for their trespasses against you. Do you think you can move forward? Why or why not?

_____

_____

5. What about you? Are you holding on to something, overanalyzing a mistake you made? What's preventing you from forgiving yourself?

_____

_____

I cannot go back and try to fix the past.
I can only make amends for what happened and claim
the forgiveness that God has ready for me.
—Suzanne Eller, quoting her friend Michelle

CHAPTER 4

The ~~Good~~ GREAT Book

The best thing to do with the Bible is to know it in the head, stow it in the heart, sow it in the world, and show it in the life.

—Unknown

At first glance, the Bible appears to be pretty overwhelming. There are lots of pages, hundreds of thousands of words, and a myriad of messages buried within, waiting to be found—uncovered, if you will. I don't know about you, but I tend to shy away from books *that* big—books that are not only going to demand a bunch of my time, but quite possibly *all* of my attention, too.

A guide of that scale? It's a lot to undertake, right? But maybe our thought process is all wrong here. Because the Bible—and what it contains—isn't a book we have to read . . . it's the book we *get* to read. The one we get to dive into . . . investigate . . . discover.

Up until this point, I haven't mentioned it all that much. Sure I've referenced Scripture as it has pertained to our topics, but I guess you could say I've been holding out—waiting/wanting to introduce you to *this* book in *this* chapter. See, the manual you currently hold in your hands is a guide to get your journey started with Christ. But the Bible? That's the book that's going to instruct you on how to live your life according to God and His plans for you.

It's *His* words, ladies. *His* accounts, *His* teachings. The Bible is God's communication with us. It's His love letter, if you will. Dr. Steven Crane, pastor at Eagle Christian Church in Eagle, Idaho, refers to this book as the Christian's constitution—our operator's manual[1] for this life we've been given and beyond. Yep. This one book will instruct you on how to follow Him heart and soul, body and mind. It will show you the greatness of God, just as it will explain the life and teachings of Christ. Despite the fact that the Bible is over two thousand years old—the information included, the words expressed, and the testimony revealed within are totally relevant, even in this day and age. Even in this broken world.

Imagine that.

Know what else? The Bible is for *you*. I can't tell you how many times I've read through a passage only to be blown away by what God was saying to me, and how that one message was exactly what I needed to hear at that given moment. If you don't know this already, you'll soon learn. No matter how much the times have changed, or what this world of ours has come to, God's Word is crucial to the lives we lead and the relationship we desire to have with Him. The living Word of God is just waiting to be opened, received, and applied.

Yes, the Bible is big. Really big, in fact. But that doesn't necessarily mean it should be overwhelming—rather, it should be exciting. The sheer volume of this book means there's much to explore and absorb. There's so much goodness waiting to be studied . . . waiting for you.

Reading the Bible

Having said all of that, I'll admit that there have been plenty of times when I've flipped through the Bible with grandiose intentions, only to sit there dumbfounded by what it was trying to tell me. In the past, I've struggled to decipher its meaning . . . to unravel what God was getting at. As a Christian newbie, it was like I needed a decoder ring, and big flashing lights to point me in the right direction—to tell me what to read, when to read it, and

> *He restores the soul when sin is confessed. He gives wisdom and strength in times of discouragement. He fills up the life of his child with his joy as he has fellowship with his own (John 15:11; 1 John 1:3).*
> **—Moody Bible Institute**

how to translate the depth of the message lying within Scripture. I wanted to engage with those words, but kept getting lost in the text. I didn't know who was what, when things took place, how to pronounce half of the names, and found myself missing the significance of the words by getting caught up in the logistics of it all. I didn't know the difference between the Old Testament and the New, and was wondering why there was God and then Jesus as well. And somehow there was a Holy Spirit involved in the mix, too? Girls, I wanted to apply this book to my life. I was hungry for its meaning. I needed its encouragement, just as I desperately wanted to understand it—to know it.

Instead I grew slightly frazzled and pretty frustrated—and rather than getting sucked in to that bestseller, I found myself putting it down instead. Oy.

The Bible can indeed be complicated at times. As Dr. Crane points out,

> Every book of the Bible was written for a specific audience. Part of understanding the Bible is finding out what it meant to the original audience in their setting. You must find out to whom it was written, why it was written, and what did it mean to them. Only after understanding what it meant to the original audience can we find meaning and application today.[2]

Now, I don't share this with you in order to deter you from reading the Bible—quite the opposite in fact. I'm telling you this so that when you sit down with God's Word, you are better prepared, you know what to expect, and you can get the most out of the time spent with Him. I want you to be ready to embrace these Scriptures, peel back their layers, and rid yourself of any confusion right from the very start.

I want you to be able to open the Bible and never want to put it down.

Shakespeare and Christ

Shakespeare and Christ?! You're probably thinking that I've lost it at this point. After all, what could these two people possibly have in common? This was the question my fellow parishioners encountered during a Sunday morning sermon delivered by pastor Steven Crane. As most sat in their seats attempting to ponder the commonalities of these two, Dr. Crane continued his talk by asking the following question: "Do you remember listening to Shakespeare for the first time?" As I thought back to my own experience with English literature during my freshman year of high school, I can clearly recollect my introduction to William Shakespeare. For most of us, *Romeo and Juliet* was required reading in our formative (and oh-so-fun) pubescent years. However, the reason I can vividly recall this play from my random stash of memories, is because I had no idea what *that* piece of literature was trying to say; I just didn't get it.

> *All Scripture is breathed out by God and profitable for teaching, for reproof, for correction, and for training in righteousness, that the man of God may be complete, equipped for every good work.*
> **—2 Timothy 3:16–17** ESV

Shakespeare was difficult to relate to, his words were foreign, his writing archaic. The guy didn't speak my language, and I found myself confused (and slightly annoyed) when attempting to figure out what he was trying to say—without using crib notes or a cheat sheet, that is. My confusion stemmed from the fact that I was reading these works through my twentieth-century mind. The dialect just didn't make sense because Shakespeare's works came from a completely different era. But as I continued reading (under duress, I might add), I began to understand a little bit more. The language he used started to make sense and after enough exposure to it, the intentions and the depth of this man's writing were slowly revealed. And you know what? I actually enjoyed it. No really. It appeared I just needed to acquaint myself with Shakespeare's slang in order to locate the brilliance within.

The Bible is much the same way.

Once you begin studying the contents of this book, and familiarizing yourself with its messages, you'll begin to see that the language of the Bible will become recognizable. The words within aren't intended to be glanced over, but studied. God's message isn't meant to go in one ear and out the other; it's to be absorbed, memorized, and applied.

> Like any work of ancient literature, one must learn the culture, customs, and vocabulary to understand it. Parts of the Bible are complicated, but the more you read, study, and learn, the more beautiful it becomes. (Steven A. Crane)

The Bible isn't your average book. It takes time to read. It takes effort, thought, and application, too. It takes a commitment.

But let's be honest—wouldn't it be easier to shy away from its contents, to leave it unopened . . . undiscovered? As far as seeking a relationship with Christ, couldn't the Bible be optional? Skipped over? Not this time . . . not when it comes to a deeper understanding of God and His Son. See, most of us desire an instruction book for life. Especially as a mom, all I've wanted for the past ten years of motherhood is for someone to lay it all out there for me—to tell me what to do and provide me the information on how to do it. Most (if not all of us) seek direction to show us the way—a book we can follow. Friends, the Bible is that book, and more. It is the manual we all yearn for. It is our field guide through life. Every message we need to hear, every tool we need to apply is in there.

But I know what you're thinking, just as I'm aware of what you might've heard, too: *how can we believe (you know—like with our whole being) what the Bible states? How can we hold it as truth?*

The way to have Christ in mind—is to know His Word by heart.
—Ann Voskamp

Believing the Bible

It's just a fairytale—a collection of stories bearing no truth at all.

It's a farce, not to be believed. The Bible stretches the truth.

There are parts of the Bible that may have happened, but for the most part, I don't trust what it says.

Have you heard any of these statements before? Or, have *you* made any of these claims about the Bible yourself?

I have.

I've literally thought (or spoken) all of these words at one time or another. The worst part? I'd never even read the Bible before stating my opinion of it. I'd never taken the time to open that book and disprove the allegations I was making against it. Prior to becoming a Christian, I didn't care enough to find out.

Is it surprising?

Not at all.

Girls, I've heard the Bible likened to mythology, folklore, and yes, make-believe. And as a new Christian unsure of how to defend my Savior's honor, I stood there quiet—not knowing what to say, how to interject, or how to present biblical truths to another. Instead, I said nothing . . . I did nothing.

Let me tell you, a quiet Christian is a sure sign that an opportunity's been missed. And it had been. But I don't want you to make the same mistake. Not at all. So, in preparation for writing this book, I began conducting some research of my own, and stumbled upon a great read titled, *How to Grow in Your Christian Life.*[3] In it, I found a number of ways to not only defend the Bible but to equip you with the basic facts and principles relating to it. I wanted to present these ideas so that you would be more informed and better prepared when it came to defending the Bible, God, Christ, and the Holy Spirit—and when it comes to protecting this newfound faith. Besides, you're looking for answers, right? You're seeking the truth, am I correct?

Take this in, friends . . .

1. Can we believe the Bible?

The Bible is *the* Word of God, and tells us that if we believe in Christ as our Savior, we will inherit eternal life (John 5:24). The Bible has been written to give us assurance of that life. But how do we hold it as truth or place our trust in it? Here are some facts you might be interested in knowing:

- **The Bible has stood the test of time.** False teachings, paganism, atheism, and whatever else that has threatened to destroy the Word of God have all failed. True story.
- **The Bible is historic.** God spoke through different men, languages, walks of life, occupations, and in varying countries, over a 1600-year time span; the Bible is in fact the Word of God (2 Pet. 1:21).
- **The Bible provides proof.** Archaeology confirms ruins (for example the walls of Jericho) verifying biblical record—just one of many proofs that the biblical record is true.
- **The Bible denounces evil and all sin.** Sin is neither hidden nor tolerated in the Holy Scriptures. We see this through the example of Moses where God faithfully portrayed his failures as well as his obedience.
- **The Bible has the ability to change lives.** The words contained in the Scriptures offer eternal salvation. We know that we can be saved by believing (John 5:24).

*Note: See page 226 for more information.

2. Why should we read the Bible?

If the above answers weren't enough to get you interested in at least purchasing a Bible of your own, hopefully the information provided here will.

• **For correction.** The Word of God is necessary for spiritual correction. The Bible is our manual for life and the afterlife. It's the guide we need in order to understand how to receive salvation, and develop a fellowship with God and His Son, Jesus Christ. The tools and instruction we need reside in that book.

• **For counsel.** Life is hard. You're already quite aware of this fact, am I right? There are things that go on in our lives that we don't have answers for: too many twists, way too many turns, and not enough answers. How we respond and how our faith deepens because of these trials is the real test. The Bible is there to provide counsel in times of trial.

• **For warfare.** Wait, what? Warfare? The Enemy enjoys nothing more than to prey upon, tempt, and destroy God's children. The Word of God and our faith in Him is the Christian's armor against Satan, his attacks, and his nasty temptations.

• **For fellowship.** Reading the Word of God is how we are better able to know Him. He's in those pages. His wisdom, knowledge, counsel, accounts, and love are right there for us to read. Better yet, they are there for us to study, learn with other brothers and sisters in Christ, and uncover the deep-rooted messages that lie within.

3. How does one read the Bible?

• **Find a quiet place.** Secure a space somewhere within your home, car, or other spot where interruptions aren't likely to happen. Turn off your cell phone, shut down your computer, and ready yourself for a session with God.

- **Develop a routine.** Establish a time each day to devote to God. For many of us, this is the hardest thing to do, due to our schedules and the amount of sheer chaos that goes on in our daily lives. But once a routine is developed, it's much easier to adhere to.

- **Expectancy.** Girls, when you sit down to read the Bible, you should have an air of expectancy about you. Make it your goal to meet Christ personally, to know God better, to experience His words fully. Ask Him to show you your sin, beg for His will, and enjoy His fellowship.

- **Pray.** Prior to opening your text for the day, pray for God to open your eyes to His words. Pray for a deeper relationship with Him, undistracted fellowship, and further knowledge of the message being read.

- **Take it all in.** Read with a purpose. The Bible is not the sort of book that can be glanced at or read through at a quick pace. It is meant to be reflected on, studied, and applied. You may find that you like reading only one verse at a time; or reading whole passages and chapters might appeal to you more. Do what works for you.

- **Let it sink in.** "God's word is alive and speaks powerfully if we will give it time to sink in."[4] Start your readings with short passages or enlist the help of a devotional to guide you through the Bible. Allow God to speak to you personally with a suggested reading. Write down notes in the margin of your Bible; study the meaning of each passage and how it can be applied to your current situation and your life.

- **Apply it.** Memorize Scripture, witness to others about your findings, and use what you have learned in your daily encounters (on your own or with others). The Bible is to be used and applied to your life each and every day.

Further, I think it's helpful to know (and this may be news to you), that the Bible isn't laid out in chronological order. Instead, it is grouped by topic, which means that it doesn't

> *The Bible is the portrait of Jesus Christ.*
> **—John Stott**

matter where you start reading, as long as you read. But if you want a great place to start, try John, James, or Mark. Target a reading plan that begins with the Gospels and get to know Christ, His life, and His teachings. For your convenience, I've included a number of links to Bible-reading plans in Part Four of this book, to get you started on your walk through His Word.

So, what do you think? Still need more answers? Still stuck doubting the contents of the Bible? Hey, I've spent many a moment grappling with these very ideas and principles. The world was telling me one thing and the Bible was asking me to believe another . . . and I needed to find out the truth.

Once and for all.

Q & A

You're curious. You want answers to the pressing questions you've got looming in the back of your mind. You want someone to tell it to you straight. And as a woman concerned with pursuing her faith passionately, it's only right that you hear the truth. Because there's no going about this sort of relationship halfway: it's all or nothing from here on out.

When I first began my walk, I wanted to know *everything* contained in that Bible. Everything! I wanted to be able to sit down with a pastor, and bombard him with questions. One after another. I wanted to learn. To engage. I desired to soak it all in. However, based upon my previous church experiences I encountered as a youth, I considered it taboo to request such info from a clergyman. Odd, right? Like I'd get reprimanded for doing so or something. But you know what I finally figured out? The only dumb question is the one that's never asked. So, I put my past issues aside and chatted with Dr. Steven Crane in order to help clarify some of the confusion I was feeling . . . the same bewilderment you might be in the grips of right now. Dr. Crane has published several books on theology and I consider him to be thoroughly knowledgeable when it comes to all things biblically related.

I devised ten questions about the Christian faith, the Bible, as well as the Trinity (Godhead) that so many of us desire more information on. Here are some answers, girls.

1. How do I know God is even real? What caused God?

Everything that has a beginning needs a cause. Every finite, contingent thing needs a cause. But God does not have a beginning, or a cause—because God is infinite. God is the "uncaused." The very word for God used in Scripture is the "I am"—the always existent one. We can't ask what caused God, because God is infinite.

2. Between the Old Testament and the New Testament, God appears very different. It's as if He goes from being harsh to loving. How do you explain this?

The same loving God is spoken of in both the Old and New Testament. "The LORD is gracious and compassionate, slow to anger and rich in love. The LORD is good to all; he has compassion on all he has made" (Ps. 145:8–9).

While it is true that the Old Testament contains more stories of God's judgment than the New Testament does, the Old Testament covers a span of over four thousand years, while the New Testament takes place over less than a hundred.

God is said to be both loving and holy throughout the Bible.

3. Are the Ten Commandments still relevant?

The answer is yes! The Ten Commandments are still relevant to our world—extremely relevant. But they have also been replaced by something better than the rule of law.

At the heart of your question is the issue of salvation. Under the New Covenant (forecast in Old Testament Scripture in Jeremiah 31:31), emphasis is not on what we must do (keeping the law), but on what Christ has done for us. The emphasis is not on the works we must perform, but on the righteousness Jesus is able to produce in us. By Jesus' perfect work on the cross, He has rescued and saved us from sin. Salvation can only come one way: not through the law, but through the grace of Jesus Christ.

4. What am I supposed to do when my doubts about God surface?

Everyone (preachers included) experiences doubt from time to time. Doubting does not have to destroy faith. The strongest faith is one which has resolved doubts. For Christian faith to be credible faith, it must be an examined faith. I am a Christian minister precisely because I have wrestled with doubt and have determined Christianity credible.

Furthermore, doubt does not equate to unbelief, nor is it the opposite of faith. Doubt wants to, and even will, believe—if there is sufficient evidence. A person should do whatever they can to resolve doubts in order to make a strong, informed decision about Christ.

5. Where did the dinosaurs come into play? How come the Bible doesn't talk about this?

Actually, the Bible does mention creatures that many believe to be dinosaurs. Job mentions the Behemoth and Leviathan. Behemoth is described as having a tail like a cedar tree (Job 40:15–19). Leviathan is pictured with scales, terrible teeth, and is so fierce that no one dares to wake him (Job 41). Some older versions of the Bible call them "dragons."

6. Is Christianity the one true religion? What about all the other types of faith out there?

After an examination of all the facts, I am convinced that the Bible is accurate and that Jesus is indeed the Son of God. I believe that Jesus came to earth, lived as a man, and died for our sins to provide reconciliation with God. I have become convinced by the "truth" of His words when He says, "I am the way, the truth, and the life. No one comes to the Father except through Me" (John 14:6 NKJV).

Christianity proves itself trustworthy in ways that other religions and viewpoints do not.

7. What is this Trinity thing? I'm not sure I get it.

Christian belief in the unity of "three persons" in "one God" is not a contradiction. God is three persons (The Father, the Son, and the Holy Spirit), but only one in nature. The Trinity goes beyond any explanation I can give it. It goes beyond reason without going against reason. I believe in the Trinity, not because I understand it but because it's biblical.

Someone once said, "If we try to understand God completely, we may lose our mind. But if we do not believe in the Trinity, we may very well lose our soul."

8. Tell me about evolution. How does it play into Christianity? Who's right? Who's wrong?

I don't have enough faith to be an evolutionist. Here are some of my arguments:

- Evolution does not explain where stuff comes from. Nothing times nothing (no matter how many years you throw at it) still equals nothing.
- The principle of irreducible complexity destroys evolution. Are there mechanisms in life that cannot be explained by a series of individual mutations? Stated another way, are there life systems that must have developed simultaneously in an advanced manner for creatures to survive (think blood clotting, eyesight, hearing, etc)?
- I also love what is called by creationists, "the appearance of age." If the biblical account is accurate, on the first day of Adam's existence, did he look like an infant or a man? On the first day of a tree's existence did it have rings or was it a twig? On the first day of existence, could a rock be carbon-dated accurately?
- If you look around you, do you see evidence of design in the world in which we live? If there is design, there must be a designer.

9. Are aliens real? Are we alone in this world or are there other civilizations?

My honest answer is "I dunno." The Bible makes no claim one way or another. I would answer that it is certainly possible that God could create another universe with an inhabitable planet but we get no clear indication of this anywhere in Scripture.

10. Why are there various translations of the Bible? Which one are we to follow and why?

Any attempt to translate from one language to another is difficult. There are not always exact, word-for-word equivalents. Sometimes it takes several words to translate a single word, and sometimes many words can be translated with a single word. Also, language changes. While the King James English was widely used in the 1600s, we don't speak like that today, so updates are helpful. There are two types of translations. There are word-for-word translations (trying to find the best equivalent word, no matter how difficult this may be) and there are thought-for-thought translations (simply trying to convey the original meaning, but often using some liberties). Both can effectively communicate God's Word. I have a sermon entitled "Translation Frustration" which demonstrates this. I actually recommend both types of Bibles. For in-depth Bible study you need a literal, word-for-word translation. Two very good ones are the English Standard Version and the New American Standard Version. For devotional reading, a dynamic translation (thought for thought) can be very helpful. I like the New Living Translation. There are also paraphrased Bibles. These are not translations, but an author's attempt to recapture the message in his own words. These can be very useful, but should not be used for Bible study (The Message and The Living Bible are examples of biblical paraphrases).

The answers provided above are just the beginning when it comes to furthering your knowledge of the Bible and its contents. Friend, you're bound to have plenty more questions as you grow in your faith and further your walk. Let this chapter be your starting point to navigating the Bible in your pursuit of truth.

TESTIMONY

Timing Is Everything
Stephanie Shott

Open my eyes, that I may behold
wondrous things out of your law.
—Psalm 119:18 ESV

Through the years, many precious women have asked me: How much time should I spend in God's Word? What are some ways I can really know God? And, how can I understand the Bible more?

These are all really great questions. Questions I myself wondered about for years.

The beauty is that God created each of us very uniquely, so how we grow in our relationship with Him will be just as unique as we are. There is no one-size-fits-all kind of answer.

Some of us learn visually. We like worksheets, workbooks, videos, and lists. Others are auditory. They love deep conversations, audio books, and listening to lessons. Still others are tactile learners (hands on). They like doing all the above, but they need to take notes, too. They love making graphs, charts, and crafts that will help them make sense of what they have just read.

But no matter what your learning style or personality type is, there are a couple of spiritual disciplines that are necessary for us all to grow in our relationship with God: time in His Word and time in prayer.

Discipline. It's not a popular word in our world today. We live in a drive-thru, microwave, and Google society. We want it now and we want it our way. Well, maybe you don't, but I tend to struggle with the convenience of the instant.

For me it's been a journey of discovery. A journey that has taught me a lot about myself and a lot about how God has wired me.

So, once I honed in on what works for me, I've pretty much stuck with it through the years. Some of the seasons of my life have caused me to juggle my schedule and change my routine, but the key ingredients have virtually remained the same. I may have tossed around the order in which they fall—but there are five elements that I try to maintain as constant when it comes to my time with the Lord.

1. Pray–Prayer is how we talk to God. Reading His Word is how we hear Him speak to us. I've been in plenty of one-sided conversations before and I know it's pretty frustrating when someone dominates the conversation and you can't get a word in edgewise. I don't want to do that to the Lord. I need Him. He really doesn't need me. I'm the one who stands in need of wisdom, direction, hope, and healing. So when I pray before I read, I invite God into a conversation.

The Bible tells us in James 4:5 that He yearns for us. In a world where it's easy to feel invisible, the Creator of the universe sees us, loves us, and longs for us to spend time with Him.

And He not only sees us, but He is intimately involved in the deepest details of our lives. He knows us better than we know ourselves. He knows our greatest fears and our deepest desires. He understands our insecurities, the pain of our past, and the burdens we carry every day.

The world around us may not know we even exist, but we never escape the view of God, not even for a second.

And that God who loves us with a relentless love is the same God who says, "Come to Me, all *you* who labor and are heavy laden, and I will give you rest" (Matt. 11:28 NKJV).

So when we pray, we invite Him in to speak to us in our place of need.

2. Read and study God's Word–Great treasures and profound power are found tucked in the pages of the sacred Word of God. There's a war being waged in our hearts and minds to prevent us from believing that what God says about Himself and what He says about us are true.

But it's the Word of God that gives power and clarity to our lives—not only to what we believe but to the way we live our lives. The problem we face is that if we don't really know what the Word of God says, we can't know what is true about who we are, what our deepest needs really are, how to overcome our circumstances, and how to walk in victory.

After living through a decade of sexual abuse as a child, I was left with a really skewed view of life, love, and everything in between. I was one broken little girl who felt like my only purpose in life was to be used and abused. I believed I was a throwaway.

But when I read in God's Word that I'm more than a conqueror, that God sees me as pure and perfect just as He sees His Son, that I'm loved with an everlasting love—the apple of His eye, His pure and spotless bride—then I'm able to stand when the weight of the world comes crashing in on me. I'm able to overcome thoughts of depression and despair.

Knowing God's Word makes all the difference. It grounds you like nothing else can and equips you for the battle that rages around you, and within your own heart.

When I first became a Christian, I asked a precious man of God how I could know God and His Word more. This is the advice he gave me: "Stephanie, there's a difference between reading God's Word and studying it. And you need to do everything you can to do both every day."

That has been my quiet-time filter for much of my Christian walk.

Read it daily. It's food for your soul. Study it deeply. It's the weapon you will need for the battles you will face.

3. Journal your way through the Word–When I journal my way through the Word, it helps me be on the lookout—to listen for God's still small voice as I'm reading the written Word. Later on, I'm able to look back on the places where God has spoken to me, answered prayer, and given me wisdom and direction for the next step.

To make it easy, I just write out four headings:

1. What does God's Word say in context?
2. What is God's Word saying to me?
3. How can I apply it to my life?
4. How can I use what I've read to pray more specifically?

If you are taking the time to have a two-way conversation with God, it's a great idea to journal that time together. There's nothing quite so precious or powerful as knowing the God of all Creation speaks to you in real and practical ways.

4. Use a devotional–I love devotionals. They're short and sweet, but many of them are very powerful. They give you an opportunity to get a different perspective on things. My all-time favorite is *My Utmost for His Highest* by Oswald Chambers, but there are a ton of great devotionals that the Lord can use to speak to you in the midst of your circumstances. I've learned you have to be careful that you find one that is biblically accurate. Unfortunately, when you read other people's thoughts on God, their writing may be good—it may even be inspirational—but it might not be biblically accurate. (That's another good reason we read and study God's Word . . . so we'll know what we believe and why!)

5. Pray again–Asking God to speak to you before you read His Word is inviting Him into the conversation . . . it's asking Him to impart to you the wisdom you need from His Word. But after you've read the Word of God, and journaled your way through a specific passage, it's time to bask in the beauty of His presence, to worship Him, to come to Him with thanksgiving and praise, to cast your cares upon Him, to seek His face for your needs and the needs of those you love, to repent of any sins you may have in your life, and to call upon Him to help you walk by faith and not by sight.

Knowing God more happens when we spend time with Him in the Word and in prayer. It really is as simple (and as hard) as that! It's about being disciplined because you value that time as priceless.

But you also have to give yourself some leeway. Life happens and circumstances don't always add up to an hour in the morning reading God's Word and an hour in the evening studying it. People get sick. Tragedy strikes. Schedules are altered. Children are up all night throwing up. Elderly parents need to be cared for. Newborn babies cry through the night. A house full of children makes it impossible to find a quiet place.

We're all in different seasons in our lives and we face an ongoing jockeying of our schedules while we desperately try to prevent our worlds from colliding with our time in the Word.

On the flip side of the circumstantial coin, it's important that we don't let our daily circumstances dictate our agendas. If we're not careful, our lives can become an excuse for not spending time in the Word of the Living God.

So, if you're looking for ways to make time in the Word a priority in your life, here are some ideas that I hope will inspire you.

Choose a plan. I recommend you try beginning with a "read the Bible in a year" plan now. That normally takes about twenty to thirty minutes a day.

Commit to a time frame that works for you. Evaluate your schedule and write down your time in the Word in your appointment book. That's right—make an appointment with God and guard it at all possible costs.

Be accountable. Find a friend who loves to spend time in the Word and give her permission to keep you accountable.

Teach someone. You will never learn more than when you teach someone else. Teaching puts you under the gun and literally makes you spend time in the Word. I've often said that speaking is selfish for me because it motivates me to diligently study God's Word so that I'm able to present it clearly to others.

Be forgiving. Give yourself room to fail and room for life to happen without beating yourself up or giving up. If you miss a day, a week, a month . . . just look at your plan and begin reading where you are. Don't try to catch up . . . just start where you are and get back on track.

Be diligent to present yourself approved to God, a worker who does not need to be ashamed, rightly dividing the word of truth.
—**2 Timothy 2:15** NKJV

Psalm 119:92–93 reminds us of the life-giving qualities of God's Word: "Unless Your law had been my delight, I would have perished in my afflic- tion. I will never forget Your precepts, [how can I?] for it is by them You have quickened me (granted me life)" (AMP).

If you struggle with trying to figure out how much time is enough, just remember, when it comes to the time we spend in God's Word, there is no such thing as "too much."

I'm hoping this chapter has brought you the support needed in order to silence some of your doubts, bring inner peace, and fur- ther solidify your trust in God's Word—the Bible. Please know, the Bible isn't meant to be read front to back, cover to cover, nor is it designed with the purpose of reading just once. The Bible isn't about getting through, it's about getting into. Rather than thumbing through its contents, or adding it to the library of books currently collecting dust on our shelves, this manuscript for our lives is meant to be used over and over again . . . daily in fact. Its pages are meant to be highlighted, just as its cover beckons to be worn from use.

Furthermore, the verses studied are intended for memorization. They are to be carried with us—stored in our hearts, fresh on our lips, and at the forefront of our minds. What better way to infuse God's Word into our lives (and share it with others) than to know it both inside and out?

Your word is *a lamp to my feet and a light to my path.*
—Psalm 119:105 NKJV

. . . .

Prescription for Praise

 READ:

The Bible (Use one of the plans in the back of this book, or an audio or online version—there are many guides to reading and studying the Bible; the important thing is to find one that works for you.)

Jesus Calling by Sarah Young (or other devotional)

NET Bible (New English Translation; find a link to read it online at netbible.com)

How to Study the Bible by Watchman Nee

Bible Study Corner (www.biblestudycorner.com)

A Woman's Guide to Reading the Bible in a Year by Diane Stortz

A Modern Girl's Guide to Bible Study by Jen Hatmaker

Know Your Bible by Paul Kent

Dear Jesus by Sarah Young

 STUDY:

Matthew 4:1–11

Psalm 119:9

John 4:23

John 16:13

John 15:11
2 Peter 1:21
2 Peter 3:2, 15–16
Hosea 1:1
Ezekiel 1:3
Exodus 24:4
2 Timothy 3:16–17
John 14:6

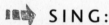 SING:

"God's Not Dead" performed by Newsboys
"Creed" performed by Third Day
"Glorious Day" performed by Casting Crowns
"Shout to the Lord" performed by Darlene Zschech
"Born Again" performed by Newsboys
"Word of God Speak" performed by MercyMe
"Thy Word" performed by Michael W. Smith and Amy Grant

APPLY:

1. What is the difference between the Old and New Testaments? How many books are in the Bible?

_____

_____

2. Who were the apostles? Why were they important?

_____

_____

3. Why are there various translations of the Bible? Google it and write your answer here.

_____

_____

4. Why would it be of value to the reader to "peel back the layers of Scripture"? What does this mean?

_____

_____

5. How do you plan to read the Bible? What steps will you take to memorize Scripture and incorporate God's words into everyday life?

_____

_____

*Don't let the noise of the world keep you
from hearing the voice of the Lord.*
—Unknown

Notes:
1 Steven A. Crane, *Email "Messages": A Minister Responds to Questions from His Congregation* (Eugene, OR: Wipf and Stock, 2011), 45.

2 Steven A. Crane, "Taking a Stand for the Bible" (sermon, Eagle Christian Church, Eagle, ID, September 15, 2013).

3 Moody Bible Institute, *How to Grow in Your Christian Life*, First Steps for the New Christian (Nashville, TN: Cumberland House, 2002; first published 1957 by Moody Bible Institute).

4 Ibid.

CHAPTER 5

Livin' on a Prayer

To pray is to let go and let God take over.

—Unknown

Hey God,

I guess I don't know what to say. Here I am, kneeling before you with a heavy heart, so confused, scared, and uneasy about this life I'm living . . . this path I'm taking. At times, it seems right. But in other moments, I feel as though I have no idea what I'm doing, or whether I'm living as you intended. God, there's so much uncertainty for me right now and I need to feel you close. I know you hear me, but at this moment, I need to feel your arms around me—because the season I'm in just won't let up . . . it's as if I can't break free.

As for my surroundings? Lord, the world is closing in. I'm well aware that I need to live for the next life—for the day when we meet face to face. I understand that this life is temporary, but I can't help myself from getting wrapped up in it. I feel so human. So flawed. So sinful in my nature. So unsure.

I just ask that you be with me, dear Lord. Strengthen me. Give me the courage to follow you with my entire being. Enhance my faith so that I might have the relationship I so desperately desire with you.

God, hear my prayers.

Going through the Motions

When was the last time you prayed? I mean *reeeeally* prayed? As in, got-on-your-knees-and-bared-your-soul-to-God kind of praying? Can you recall when you last sent some praise His way, told Him thanks, or just said hey?

The concept of prayer had always been a bit foreign to me. I was never really sure what a discussion with God was supposed to sound like, how long it needed to be . . . or how often I had to do it. I knew I was *supposed* to pray, but I didn't really understand why, or what the point of it was. I wasn't sure who benefited from this form of communication either—was it me? Or God? And were the words I was extending even being received . . . *heard*?

So I prayed because I felt like I *had* to.

I told God what I thought He wanted to hear. I thanked Him for my blessings, threw out a few signs of the cross, and then wrapped up the convo in order to grab some shut-eye. I didn't stop to listen. I didn't wait for an answer either. I said my piece and left it at that.

When it came to a prayer life, I didn't really have one. That's right. It appeared I was just going through the motions.

> *Spending time with God puts everything else in perspective.*
> **—Unknown**

I prayed every day, in the same location, using the same words. I folded my hands, closed my eyes, and repeated matching pleas night after night. Never once did I praise Him. Never once did I tell Him I loved Him either. My prayer life was disconnected because I was. I hadn't yet realized that the act of prayer wasn't meant to be a series of calculated, well-thought-out words I *thought* He'd enjoy hearing—rather, they needed to be an extension of what He already saw in my heart (Ps. 95:2).

What I was unable to comprehend at the time was that God was much more concerned with *why* I was praying, *what* I was saying, and the state of my heart, than He was with the ritualistic efforts I was putting forth. I was a girl who prayed out of fear, not love. I prayed to keep the comfortable life I was living, along with the safety and security I'd grown accustomed to. My desires were for my will to win out—to get my way—what I wanted. I never opened a Bible, never sought Him through Scripture, nor understood the importance of doing so.

Worse, those "chats" with my heavenly Father were all about me—my wants and desires. I considered prayer to be an opportunity of sorts . . . the chance to bow before God, and ask for all of those things I felt I deserved in my life.

God, please don't let me fail my history test. God, please allow me to perform well during my next softball game. God, please let that cute boy in geometry class like me. Oh, and I really want a new car—can you send me one? You get the picture. But God isn't Santa Claus, just as Christ isn't the Easter Bunny. Prayer isn't about wishing and wanting. It's about soul searching. It's about our devotion to our Creator. And it's about relationship.

Do you understand the difference? Do you see prayer for what it really is—the catalyst for a deep connection with our Father—and why that's even necessary? I now look at this discipline as my opportunity to connect with Him, show gratitude, repent of my sins, listen for His cues, and be in His presence. As long as I am real with the Lord, honest, truthful, consistent, and genuine, then my prayer life is right on track. You see, I had to learn to make time for God, I had to learn how to communicate with Him.

I had to invite Him in.

Dear God: An Invitation

> *Let us then approach God's throne of grace with confidence, so that we may receive mercy and find grace to help us in our time of need.*
> **—Hebrews 4:16**

As I've already mentioned, prayer is many things. It's an expression of love to our heavenly Father, appreciation for the blessings we've been given, as well as the chance for confession and praise. But prayer also serves as an invitation—an opportunity to ask God into our lives, our minds, our souls. It's bonding time. It's all of these things and more.

Still, not everyone does it. Not everyone gets it.

Hey, can I ask you a question? When you hear of a tragedy, an unfortunate event, or something that's far beyond your control, what do you do? Upon learning such information—scared, feeling alone, unaware of what steps to take next—what's the first action you take? For most of us, the answer is prayer. It's in those precise moments when we hit our knees, beg God for a different outcome, and plead with Him to be near. It's during those unbearably hard moments when we cry out for His help and ask for His intervention. It's right then and there that we seek Him out and search for His presence. But why don't we do this all of the time? Why do most of us only consult God when we're in trouble, scared, or hurt?

Ladies, we don't need a tragedy to occur for us to seek God's will and counsel. We don't need formal appeals or even memorized devotions to approach His throne either. Know what else? It doesn't matter where you pray—whether it's in front of your friends at lunch, in the privacy of your own home, or even in the middle of rush-hour traffic. God is ready, waiting, and listening anytime you want to talk.

So why should we pray?

I pray because I believe in the Word of God, as well as the sacrifice that Christ made for my salvation. I know that living this life without the Trinity (God, Jesus, and the Holy Spirit) just isn't for me. I've tried it! God was in His place and I was in mine and let me tell you, it

> *I pray because I can't help myself. I pray because I'm helpless. I pray because the need flows out of me all the time—waking and sleeping. It doesn't change God—it changes me.*
> **—C. S. Lewis**

didn't work out too well. It wasn't until I invited Him into my heart that life became clearer and the larger picture came into focus. Girls, I pray because I'm not strong enough to deal with this world and the events life throws my way (on my own). Not without God. I pray because there's power in doing so.

TESTIMONY

Unanswered Prayers
Jennifer Dukes Lee

I'm afraid of messing this up.

That's the thought running through my mind as I recline in the bed next to my daughter, who catapults hard questions into the inky hollowness above us.

I can't see her tears, but I can hear them. It's the way her tiny voice wobbles and squeaks. I reach along my side to find her hand in the dark.

"Why doesn't God answer my prayers, Mom?" She snaps out the words, like they're hot, like she has to spit them out before they burn. "Doesn't He hear me?"

I let out my breath in one steady stream, into the quiet above her polka-dotted comforter, begging silently for some shred of inspiration that I can offer to a ten-year-old girl who is asking the hardest questions.

The only words I can find hover like useless syllables above us: "I don't know, Lydia. I just don't know. I don't know. I don't."

I blink back my own tears. I want to offer more. I am her mother, the one she is trusting tonight with the answers. And this is it? A series of *I don't knows*?

Truth is, I've uttered the same questions in those moments when my prayers boomeranged back without the answers I begged for. I've pounded my fists into armchairs and bed pillows and the carpet when God hasn't acted the way I wanted Him to.

I've hurled furious questions into the darkness, too. Lydia's voice wobbles again: "I'm angry, Mom. Sometimes, I'm angry at God. Do you think He's mad at me when I say that? Will He still love me?"

I turn on my side and rub her cheek. I do know the answer to this one: "God loves you. Always. And Lydia, don't you ever forget it. You promise? No matter the pain, or the heartache, or the mystery of this world. No matter if you can't see one step in front of you, or if you can't make sense of anything behind you, He always loves you. He loved you all the way to the cross and back. And that, my daughter, is a promise I believe with every ounce of my life."

I keep caressing that soft cheek. And we let the answers hang there awhile.

It's a bittersweet moment.

Sweet, because this is what I've always wanted: honest exchanges about faith with my two daughters. I've never wanted them to be ashamed of their questions, or to feel the need to sugarcoat their feelings, or to shellac their ache with clichés. I've only wanted them to be gut-level honest with a God who knows what they're feeling anyway.

But it's bitter, too. Bitter because of the pain that led to these honest questions that she casts out into the dark. She's ten, but she has seen how the unthinkable happens to vulnerable people in a crooked world:

- One of our daughters' young friends recently died.
- A young Haitian boy we love has been very ill.
- And in two days, Lydia will return to the operating room. Back in April, she had a skin graft to cover a hole in her eardrum. The surgery failed. And she's scared to go back.

Here in the dark, she reminds me how we had prayed together, right here in this bed, for a successful surgery. Did God not hear those prayers? That's the question she wants the unvarnished answer to. And what about when Jesus said that whatever we ask in prayer, if we believe, we will receive?

In moments like these, I freeze on the inside, and I become self-focused enough to think that my words will make or break something. Like, if I say the right or wrong thing, she'll gain—or lose—another ounce of confidence in her Father.

As if it were entirely up to me.

I am only beginning to learn that it might be okay to whisper a raspy "I don't know" into the dark (especially in these moments when I actually don't know). And I'm beginning to wonder if every "I don't know" carries more light into the dark places than the clichéd answers I've picked up along the way.

I've also learned to embrace the doubts, because—odd as it might seem—they've been the starting blocks in my own race for truth. Many years ago, at a point when I was crippled by doubt, I highlighted these words in my study Bible: "Silent doubts rarely find answers." Back then, I had just begun to ask questions of myself, and of God. In that exchange, God and I began to develop a relationship of trust. I came to understand that God wouldn't ostracize or punish me for my questions. Instead, He has been a patient friend, continually keeping the door open for more conversation.

I've also learned to invest valuable time looking in the rearview mirror of my life, reflecting back to see where God's hand was working all along in places I couldn't see when my present pain clouded my vision.

And, as Philip Yancey said, "I have learned that faith means trusting in advance what will only make sense in reverse."

Even in reverse, not everything makes sense right away. We might have to get to heaven before we find out the answers to some of our most pressing questions. For years, I have written some of those unknowns on little slips of paper, filing them in a manila envelope labeled "My Mystery File."

Lydia's surgery? Tonight, it feels like Mystery File material. But in three days? It might make total sense. We'll have to wait and see. That's what I tell my daughter in the dark.

I tell her we may have to look in the rearview mirror to see where God was working all along. Until that moment of clarity, it's okay to say "I don't know" or "God, I don't get this."

Lydia and I are learning that faith has less to do with what we understand and more to do with what Jesus Christ undertook.

Indeed, personal suffering can lead the thoughts of a believing child and her mama back to a Savior who fully grasped pain at its most unfathomable level. And that part I do understand. Even if it's just a small beginning, a little light, enough to see in the dark.

And I think Lydia understands, too—that if Jesus loved us enough to die for us, He won't abandon us in the middle of our toughest questions.

We say our prayers, and I kiss her good-night, and we know that even if we don't have answers when the sun rises tomorrow, we will still have a trustworthy God.

Praying for Others

"I'll pray for you."

From the instant this phrase was uttered, I wasn't sure if I had heard her right. Or what the gal who had hurled those words my way actually meant. So, I did what any newbie in her faith would do: I glanced behind me to see if she was talking to someone else. As I suspected, there was no one there. She was speaking to me.

Pray for me? I thought.

That was a new one. A phrase I'd never heard before and since she was directing her words my way, I needed to quickly figure out a way to respond.

> *Jesus hears us.*
> **—J. C. Ryle**

But before I could form a word, before I could politely decline her offer, I felt her hand upon my shoulder as her eyes closed, her head bowed, and she went to bat for me in front of the Lord. My first inclination was to back away and dodge the whole situation—to get out of there and replace those awkward feelings with more familiar ones. But as the rest of the group soon followed her lead, I bowed my head and accepted their pleas on my behalf.

You see, I was that fresh face at church, sitting in a Bible study class, attempting to share in a conversation. Issues were lying heavy on my heart that day so when the leader of our group asked how I was doing, I couldn't bottle my emotions any longer. I vented, let loose . . . and watched as my small group gathered around me to pray.

Me!

> *Therefore, confess your sins to one another and pray for one another, that you may be healed. The prayer of a righteous person has great power as it is working.*
> **—James 5:16** ESV

It made me uncomfortable at first. A slew of people hovering, placing their hands on my shoulders, offering up loving words to our Father. I didn't know how to take it. But as I stood there with my eyes closed, listening to their prayers and words of encouragement, I was moved. These people weren't requesting anything for themselves. Instead they were concerned with my well-being, and my family's. They were leading by example. Doing the Lord's work. They were showing me the power of prayer.

And it finally began to sink in.

As the body of Christ, we pray for one another. We pray for each other's struggles, what lies on another's heart, what pains them, and what fears they're battling against. We pray for the plight of other countries, whole populations of people, the state of the world, our husbands, our children, family members, world leaders, the persecuted church, those who have done us wrong— and the list goes on and on. Simply stated: as Christians, we pray for everything and everybody. It's where we draw strength, where we meet God, and where our faith gets put into action.

Oh, and we pray for His will to be done throughout it all.

However, not everyone agrees with this concept. Not everyone understands. Many aren't really sure how to take it when the statement *I'll pray for you* gets sent their way. Some are offended (we're talkin' totally put off) by the very idea of it. Recently, I came into contact with such a person—a self-proclaimed atheist who left a negative review on a Christian book I had just finished reading. It was a mean-spirited attack suggesting that the very idea of prayer was ridiculous. Pointless, in fact. He even went on to suggest that the act of prayer was a complete waste of time, and wasn't quite sure why anyone would give that "Invisible Guy in the Sky" a moment of their time.

Whoa.

I have to admit, I was pretty angered by this man's attack against God, but in the moments after reading his review, I couldn't help but feel unbelievably sad for him. I felt the anger come through in his words . . . the torment, too. He was a man conflicted, fighting against a relationship, spitting out hatred, but all the while (deep down), he had to know. He had to be aware of his Creator, albeit fearful and possibly afraid of what to do with such knowledge.

So, I felt the need to write him—to engage—to comment on that review, and let him know that I was indeed praying for him. I wanted this guy to know that someone actually cared, and I secretly hoped that this little interaction we were having would spark some sort of change deep within his soul. His response? "Pray for yourself and don't insult me."

> *Our prayers may be awkward. Our attempts may be feeble. But since the power of prayer is in the One who hears it and not in the one who says it, our prayers do make a difference.*
> —**Max Lucado**

Friends, not everyone gets it, nor do they truly understand the power that comes in praying for others as well as for ourselves . . . in seeking God out.

I couldn't help but see my former self in this guy. This small, chance encounter with a man who was defiant and detested the Lord revealed to me just how far I'd come in my own walk of faith . . . as well as the distance I still needed to go. It showed me how many are still out there in need of this message, and how strong the Enemy is when it comes to destroying souls.

But our God is so much stronger.

And our prayers help us to realize that.

Prescription for Praise

READ:

The 7-Day Prayer Warrior Experience by Stormie Omartian
Draw the Circle: The 40 Day Prayer Challenge by Mark Batterson
Prayer: The Ultimate Conversation by Charles Stanley
Prayer: Does It Make Any Difference? by Philip Yancey
The Prayer That Changes Everything by Stormie Omartian
Anything: The Prayer That Unlocked My God and My Soul by Jennie Allen
Before Amen by Max Lucado

STUDY:

Psalm 4:1
Philippians 1:3–4
1 Corinthians 1:4
Matthew 7:11
Luke 18:1
Colossians 4:2
1 Thessalonians 5:17

SING:

"You're Worthy of My Praise" performed by Jeremy Camp
"We Bow Down" performed by Twila Paris
"Lord, I Lift Your Name on High" performed by Rick Founds
"Wide As The Sky" performed by Matt Redman
"Pray" performed by Sanctus Real

▬➡ APPLY:

1. Why do you think prayer is necessary in our daily lives?

_____

_____

2. Has this chapter changed the way you view prayer in general? Explain.

_____

_____

3. What has your prayer life looked like in the past? Have you sought the Lord only in times of need? Or when you wanted something?

_____

_____

4. Can you think back to a time where a prayer went unanswered? You know—a time where you might have begged God for a specific outcome? How do you view that unanswered prayer today?

_____

_____

5. Let's close this chapter out in—what else—prayer . . .

God, I am so appreciative of all that you are, of all you have blessed me with, and for this life I've been given. I need your presence, Lord. Help me on this journey. Allow me to trust your will, and exude a faith like none I've ever known. Be close to me, walk me through this, and show me how to experience this love—how to experience you.
In Jesus' name,
Amen

Prayer is putting oneself in the hands of God.
—Mother Teresa

PART 3

Christianity and Beyond

*"Though no one can go back and make
a brand new start, ANYONE can start from
now and make a brand new ending."*
—Carl Bard

Christianity and Beyond

You and I probably come from totally different backgrounds. Our paths may have taken us in very different directions, as well. In fact, we might be two people who (on paper) have absolutely nothing in common. But you know what, friend? If I know anything, it's this: each of us has a story, a testimony, and a past to contend with. Each of us has had our share of pain, heartache, and struggle, too. Indeed, each and every one of us—no matter where we live, what we look like, or how our lives have transpired—well, we're all in need of a Savior.

Know what else?

You and I (inclusive of all of our differences) were made to meet right here in these pages. We were meant to take this walk *together*.

Because we can't go back. We weren't designed to have the ability to change the past, no matter how much we'd like to. What's done is done. All we can do is move forward, set our sights above, and lean on God. We can allow those teachings of the Bible to seep in, we can change our outlook, our view, our thinking. We can find purpose and meaning. We can allow the living God to dwell within our hearts.

You and I? We can do life *better*.

And where does it all start? This journey begins by placing one foot in front of the other and following Jesus.

It begins with a walk.

> *Sometimes the smallest step in the right direction ends up being the biggest step of your life. Tiptoe if you must but take the step.*
> **—Unknown**

When I first set out on my walk with Christ, I immediately wanted to know more. I wanted to be able to take that Bible I had just purchased, hold it up to my head and allow divine osmosis to take over or something. It sounds silly, I know, but I had this insatiable appetite for spiritual knowledge. And really— how could I not? My eyes had just been opened to what this life *could* (and *should*) look like . . . and I was starving for more. Like with that craving, that thirst, that hunger I described in Chapter One, I just couldn't get enough of Jesus.

I couldn't get full.

I wanted to find others who felt the same way—to learn from them, to know them. I desired a community of people who would accept and come alongside me, and a place where I belonged. I was in search of a space where I could further my relationship with God and my walk with Jesus.

And it was then that I realized I needed a church . . . a sanctuary . . . a refuge from this world.

Hold up! *Church? Christianity?*

I know, I know—my first experiences in attending church (as a child) didn't go over all that well. However, as an adult . . . as a grown woman with a slew of problems and too many broken places to count, it was a haven I needed to seek out . . . a place I needed to give another chance.

Maybe you're feeling the same way, too.

And if you are, then there's something I need to address: You see, I could go ahead and sugarcoat the next section of this guide. I could tell you that this journey you're about to embark upon is going to be simple. I could paint a rosy picture for you depicting the happiness you'll find, the bliss that will automatically be yours, not to mention the numerous rainbows that will suddenly appear, once you decide to accept Christ. I could tell you all of this and more, but I'd be doing you a huge disservice. And here's why: Becoming a Christian isn't about wearing some sort of label. Nor is it about branding one's self with a title. Christianity is a call to action.

It's learning *from* and living *for* Jesus. It's getting to know God by learning to trust Him.

Now, if you're apprehensive, I understand. After all, there may have been a number of times in your life already when you've encountered issues with Christianity. No doubt you've heard or experienced

> *Believing the teachings of Christ is not the hard part. Living them is.*
> —**Israel Wayne**

firsthand some Christians who may not have been acting, well, Christian-like. You might be recollecting at this very moment the individuals who professed Christ and did you wrong—people who may have judged you, hurt your feelings, and made some significant mistakes. Or maybe there've been "Christians" you've watched in the news who may not have been exhibiting the love of

Christ to others. "Christians" that may have had you questioning the church as a whole and Jesus in general.

It happens.

And can I just say that many (if not all) of us who have accepted Christ have been subject to a situation like this? Now, I'm not defending their actions (at all), but what I need you to remember at this phase in your journey is that we're human first. Christian or not, we all have flaws, we sin, and no one—*no one*—is perfect. So, no matter what you've encountered or heard, or what our society collectively tells you about Christianity as a whole, I want you to make this decision for yourself. I want you to read these upcoming chapters with an open mind, and I ask that you cast your previous opinions aside. Because if this girl (yeah, me) can head back to church and thrive in a population of believers, then I think anyone can . . . and should.

Being a Christian doesn't mean I won't fall . . .
it means Jesus will catch me when I do.
—Unknown

CHAPTER 6

Getting Churched

We are spiritual contributors not spiritual consumers.
The church does not exist for us. We are
the church and we exist for the world.

—Craig Groeschel

Church.

    Church wasn't a place I visited all that often as a kid; and when I did, I spent most of my time fighting with my brother, rolling my eyes in protest, or poking fun at the music director on stage. Rather than praying for peace, or speaking words of gratitude to my Savior, I found myself pleading for time to pass quickly (like warp speed), so I could get home, take those stuffy church clothes off, and get back to the important stuff in life—like playing my video games, eating Oreos, and watching cartoons.

    Needless to say, I missed out on a lot by not understanding the purpose of going to church, or why I needed to be there in the first place.

125

Maybe you fall into the same category—wondering why you *need* to go, and why these weekly gatherings outside of your home with total strangers are even necessary. Hey, you might even be pondering why a house of worship—and its congregation of believers—would willingly choose to reunite each and every week in order to worship God *together*.

I know I questioned these ideas, too. I spent years sleeping in every Sunday morning, unaware of what the building with the stained glass windows could offer me. In fact, I'd become so consumed with my own life, that it didn't occur to me to care about the church, let alone the individuals that went there. Church was for other people, not me.

It's crazy how things change though.

It wasn't until I was emotionally desperate and spiritually destitute that I eventually found myself back in the one spot I never (as in *ever*) thought I'd return to. Yep. I took my broken self back to church . . . and it was then—at that point—that I began to appreciate why people voluntarily went there. It was there that I learned why I never wanted to spend another Sunday stuck in bed, contemplating my options on the television either. I needed church. I desired to hear God's Word, and I wanted that challenge to live my life according to His will. I wanted these people around me as well—their prayers, their knowledge, their support, and their fellowship.

There was no denying that I needed this place and you know what else? This place needed me, too.

But how does one find such a church? How do we locate a house of worship where we can feel this kind of warmth—this sense of belonging? Where we can experience spiritual growth, and maybe a warm fuzzy or two?

How does a girl find a church she can indeed call home?

Finding a Church Home

After deciding to invite God back into my life and attend church, I had no idea what to expect. After all, it was a normal Sunday (not a holiday), and they weren't passing out manuals on how to do this thing called Christianity. It was

> *You can never learn that Christ is all you need until Christ is all you have.*
> —**Corrie ten Boom**

uncharted territory for sure, but what grabbed my attention and held my focus were the teachings of Christ. It was as though I was meeting Him for the first time—sitting on the edge of my seat, hanging on to every word uttered that day. And as I eventually grew more involved in that community, attended Bible studies, and hung out with fellow believers, it was apparent more than ever how crucial God's presence in my life really was, and how necessary it would be for my bottom to remain firmly planted in those sanctuary seats.

For, like, ever.

But finding a church home? Well, I can't say I had a clue as to what I was doing. I guess I was just going by my gut—what felt right. Seriously, that reintroduction to church had me looking more like a tourist than a woman attempting to take in a sermon. I must've resembled a deer caught in the headlights on numerous occasions . . . and the reason can be chalked up to the following: there was a pastor there to greet me each and every week; there was a church bulletin filled with activities to read through and become a part of; there was a bookstore complete with a café to mingle at; just as there was a welcome center, a prayer room, a children's ministry, Bible study classes, community outreach groups, and a worship band, too.

But that wasn't all.

Aside from the number of activities taking place in that building, I couldn't help but fix my eyes on one thing in particular—the parishioners. A whole slew of people, mingling together, talking, chatting, even smiling . . . and I wanted in on it. I wanted to be a part of something much bigger than myself. This was the place I desired to stay and these were the people I wanted to know.

As a girl who hadn't necessarily flourished in a church setting before, I'd be remiss if I didn't confess that my guard was up. I guess you could say I was slightly freaked out by all of the positive energy taking place, too. In fact, there were moments when I wanted to make a mad dash back to my car and return to the comfortable and seemingly safe environment my home would provide. But for me—and the brokenness that was consuming my life—attending church wasn't really an option anymore . . . it was a requirement.

Something was keeping me there inside that building that first day and the weeks, months, and years that followed. Better yet—Someone: Jesus.

So, what steps does one take when finding a church home? What should you expect upon entering those doors? What should *you* be looking for?

I'm so glad you asked.

> *Serving our brothers and sisters, loving them, and stirring them to a greater commitment to Jesus makes the church, the bride of Christ, more attractive to the world. And she needs that.*
> —**Caleb Breakey**

Church Shopping 101

When I first heard the term "church shopping," I thought it was a joke—possibly some type of church lingo that I didn't understand, or couldn't yet relate to.

I mean, *church shopping*? Who does *that*? And why?

Here comes yet another story about when I was a child (bear with me).

When I was a kid, there wasn't such a thing as church shopping. Or if there was, I had no clue any of it was going on (shocker, I know). Sampling churches prior to placing one's membership was an act that was completely lost on yours truly. As far as I knew, the sanctuary selection process was as simple as getting out the phone book, allowing those fingers to do the walking, and picking the house of worship that was closest to your neighborhood. No testing was involved. No trial period to be concerned with either.

There was no meeting with a pastor, looking into the mission statement of the church, examining doctrine, or "testing the waters," so to speak, either. You just showed up.

Today, for the majority of nondenominational churches, it's a much different story. Believe it or not, church shopping is pretty necessary, and there are a number of things one needs to consider before placing membership.

Church Checklist

So, what should you expect when you walk through those church doors? Well, aside from emotions you'll more than likely feel, you may want to take note of the following items:

> God is not calling us
> to go to church;
> He is calling us to be
> His church, the hope
> of the world.
> **—Unknown**

[Note: These suggestions are based upon nondenominational Christian churches. Church government may vary.]

Mission Statement: Every church should have a mission statement. This statement puts in written form the organization's reason for existing, stating its purpose and the leaders' God-inspired vision for the church. It's who they are striving to be, as well as their congregation's plan to serve their parishioners and community members. It states their goal as a collective group of worshipers, and provides a glimpse into how the church plans to achieve said goals. As Paul Mondragon, the pastor from The Rock Church in Yuma, Arizona, has said, "This one statement is birthed by God in the heart of the servant leader."

Keep in mind; you'll usually find this vision plastered on every document the church puts out. From weekly bulletins to monthly newsletters, this one declaration is what your church is all about. Read it carefully and ask if you have questions.

Doctrine: This is what the church preaches and how it interprets the messages of the Bible. So understanding this is extremely important, because what you believe dictates how you act.

As a newbie to the faith, you may not know a lot about doctrine and it might seem a tad confusing at first. But it matters because church doctrine drives behaviors and actions. It's how we respond to everything. So, if you get stuck, just ask. The pastor of the church you're attending should have no problem explaining what the church believes and how it lives out its faith. After all, the Bible is pretty clear about what Christians should agree on—the deity of Jesus and the Holy Spirit, the Gospel, and the authority of the Bible are at the top of that list.

Pastors/elders: Your church will most likely have a team made up of pastors, elders, deacons, and various ministry leaders of the church. Get to know these people. Meet with them and remember: their goal is to shepherd you on your walk with God. Your salvation is of utmost importance to them. Attend a worship service and see if their preaching style appeals to you. Are they convicting, engaging, and are you learning when you listen to them? Are they relatable? These are all questions to keep in mind while "shopping."

Bible studies: We've talked about how overwhelming the Bible can be and that's why Bible studies are a significant resource for Christians who want to become more familiar with its teachings. Find out what your church is offering, how often studies are being conducted, etc. Get plugged in and connect with others in the congregation by checking into what the church can provide you in this area.

Small groups: Small groups usually meet during the week at a church member's home or in a classroom at church. These groups vary in size and membership and usually tackle a specific book of the Bible, but may also implement various Bible study courses or classes. These groups offer churchgoers the opportunity to connect with their brothers and sisters in Christ and serve to provide mutual support in many other areas of Christian life. Find out what type of small group study program your potential church provides and pursue a group that interests you. Believe me, getting immersed and involved is so important when it comes to finding a church home. It's where growth occurs, change takes place, and fellow believers become family.

Children's ministry: If you have kids, then this is an important area of church programming. Meet with the head of children's ministry, get a feel for the program, ask questions, discuss what your children will be learning and the types of programs they're offering. Got older kids? This is a crucial time to get them started in their walk. Connect with the youth pastor, discuss your concerns, and explain your desires for your kiddos.

Women's ministry: How many Bible studies does the women's ministry hold annually? What kind of groups do they offer the women of the church? What kind of events do they provide during the year? Make sure to find out all of this information and more.

Outreach: We'll be spending the next chapter discussing service within the church but you'll want to check out what your prospective place of worship provides as far as community outreach. Do they have a missions ministry program? Where do they serve? How often and in what capacities? Again, we'll explore this topic in detail in the following section, but keep this fresh in your mind when deciding on a church home.

Obviously, there are a number of things to consider prior to placing your membership. And even though it may seem a tad overwhelming right now, especially because a lot of this information might be foreign to you at this point, it's still crucial to take the time to learn about the house of worship you're considering. How do you feel when you walk in there? Can you see yourself there? Are they warm and friendly? Compassionate? Are they there to spread the love of Christ? Are they preaching the gospel? These are just a few of the questions you'll want to keep in mind as you visit various churches.

And please know that I'm not pushing you into finding a church. Instead, I want to present you with the information you'll need once you reach that point. Girls, use this chapter as a reference, and know that when you feel ready to enter the body of Christ, you'll be better prepared and one step closer to understanding how it all works.

Oh, and friend, I identify with the hesitation that comes along with this decision. Remember, I spent years (*years!*) intentionally avoiding these types of buildings. And even though I've been right where you are now and understand what it's like to have good intentions in thinking you'll attend a church service soon, sometimes those plans never come to fruition—like a New Year's resolution gone bad. "One day" turns into one week, one month, and pretty soon another year has passed and we're not anywhere closer to where we need to be. But when it comes to building that relationship with Christ, that connection with God and His community of believers—when it comes to attending church—we need to do it, girls . . . we need to find our way there.

And we need to make it a priority. We need to make that connection . . . that commitment.

TESTIMONY

A Glorious Give and Take
Kathy Howard

The call came right after dinner. Wayne's parents had been in a car accident. My father-in-law had suffered some cuts and bruises. My mother-in-law was with Jesus.

Two thousand miles stretched between our home in Alberta, Canada, and their home in Louisiana. Although we had easily made the trip two weeks earlier for Christmas, the distance now seemed insurmountable. We wanted to be there immediately, but so many things had to be done.

First, I called my friend Susan. That's all it took. Within twenty minutes, loving members of our church family filled the house to see how they could help.

Connie spent two hours on the phone with the airline making reservations and securing the compassion fare. Steve gathered the Sunday school material so he could teach Wayne's class. Susan got needed dress clothes for our son Mark. Jimmy arranged to take us to the airport. Others handled the dog, the house, and countless responsibilities from which we could not simply walk away. And in the midst of all the activity there were prayers, hugs, and tears. Within hours we were ready to travel.

In Louisiana, my father-in-law encountered the same love and care from his church family. Friends went to the hospital to bring him home. Two men stayed with him through that first night. Some of the women made sure the beds were ready for us. By the time we arrived, the kitchen and refrigerator were filled with food.

God's family surrounded us in our time of need. They overwhelmed us with love. I can't imagine enduring a trial like this without the support of other believers. Yet many Christians aren't actively connected to a local church.

Why is a local church so important? We cannot receive everything God wants to give us or be everything God wants us to be apart from a vital connection to a local body of believers. He designed the life of faith to be interdependent. Christian discipleship is intrinsically communal. Each believer is dependent on the larger group of believers for what God desires to give us and do in and through us.

God Gives to Us through the Church

When my mother-in-law died in that car accident, God used the church to comfort, love, help, and support us. Their arms were His arms. Their tears were His tears. Their strength was His strength. In that tragedy, He supplied what we needed through His people.

Giving and receiving the love of Christ in the context of His church fuels and sustains our faith. Over and over in the New Testament we see the phrase "one another" to refer to this unique relationship between believers. Here are a few examples:

- Comfort one another (2 Cor. 13:11)
- Serve one another (Gal. 5:13, 1 Pet. 4:10)
- Restore one another (Gal. 6:1)
- Bear one another's burdens (Gal. 6:2)
- Forgive one another (Eph. 4:32)
- Build up one another (1 Thess. 5:11)
- Do good to one another (1 Thess. 5:15)
- Meet one another's physical needs (James 2:15–17, 1 John 3:17)
- Pray for one another to be healed (James 5:16)
- Show hospitality to one another (1 Pet. 4:9)

God has chosen to work through the church to bless His children. If we are not connected in relationship with a body of believers, we will miss out on so much of what God wants to give us.

God Grows Us through the Church

My first grandson is two years old. Watching him grow and learn and change over the last twenty-four months has been an amazing journey. The experience is different from watching my own children grow because I saw them every day. Seeing Micah only every few weeks makes the differences more dramatic. He couldn't pull up, but now he can. He crawled to get around, but now he walks. He wasn't talking, but now he says "Nana." (That's been my favorite development!)

Micah's success with crawling and walking would be severely diminished if he didn't have all four limbs. And he wouldn't be able to talk without vocal chords. While the human body is miraculous and can rise to all kinds of physical challenges, we need every single part to optimally function like God intended.

The Bible uses the human body as a metaphor for the church. This word picture helps us better understand the interdependent nature of Christians. The church needs every part, every member of the body, to function as God intends. My favorite "body" passage is in Paul's letter to the Christians in Ephesus.

> So Christ himself gave the apostles, the prophets, the evangelists, the pastors and teachers, to equip his people for works of service, so that the body of Christ may be built up until we all reach unity in the faith and in the knowledge of the Son of God and become mature, attaining to the whole measure of the fullness of Christ.
>
> Then we will no longer be infants, tossed back and forth by the waves, and blown here and there by every wind of teaching and by the cunning and craftiness of people in their deceitful scheming. Instead, speaking the truth in love, we will grow to become in every respect the mature body of him who is the head, that is, Christ. From him the whole body, joined and held together by every supporting ligament, grows and builds itself up in love, as each part does its work. (Eph. 4:11–16)

As individual members each carry out their "God assignment" in the local church, the body grows together in health and unity. As we all continue to serve together, love each other, and encourage and challenge each other, the church will become spiritually mature. Collectively and individually, we will become more and more like Christ, the Head of the church. The church and the individual believers will be steady and strong, resistant to false teaching and battle ready to defeat Satan's scheming. And the best part is that the church will reflect Christ to a lost world.

Your full and complete spiritual growth and maturity depends on the other members of the body. And their growth and maturity depends on you. When we embrace this symbiotic relationship with other believers, we are in a place where we can receive everything God wants to give us and we can become everything God wants us to be. I don't want to miss out on any of it! How about you?

The Scoop on Sunday Service

As Kathy and I both stated, the church needs each one of us just as much as we need the church. However, walking through those sanctuary doors becomes even more difficult—not to mention intimidating—when you don't know what to expect. So, rather than have you surprised by what a church service is comprised of, and what worshipping God each weekend typically looks like, I wanted to break it down for you . . . to give you the scoop and candidly share some of my own experiences.

Aside from the main message of the sermon and the Gospel being preached, there are three areas I'd like to call your attention to: worship, communion, and time of offering.

> So I'll stand with arms high and heart abandoned, in awe of the One who gave it all.
> —**Hillsong United, "The Stand"**

Sing it Loud (A Worship Story)

My mother thought it would be a good idea.

So when I was eleven years old—and in the uncomfortable throes of puberty no less—she decided to sign me up as a cast member for a summer musical her friend was directing. It was a theater group for kids of all ages and Mom thought it'd be "just what I needed" on my summer vacation—my hiatus from school. It would fill my days, keep me out of trouble, and she was convinced I would end up loving it.

The only problem? I couldn't sing.

Let me take that back. Technically, I *could* sing but the sounds that emanated from my vocal chords weren't very pleasant. Even worse, after rehearsing all summer long, and during the first performance of *How to Succeed in Business Without Really Trying*, a fellow cast member became upset (make that *enraged*) by my lack of talent. So much so that she looked me straight in the eye—in the midst of our performance no less—broke character and pleaded with me to stop singing. Right in the middle of the show.

I was *that* bad.

So imagine my surprise—after sitting through my first church service—to realize that singing wasn't all that optional. I would in fact *have* to use my voice. The girl who was once told to zip her lips (me) would *have* to attempt to carry a tune in front of others. But here's the thing: even though I might've been deemed the worst singer on the planet (just ask "Susie Langely" from my summer musical days—name protected for obvious reasons), it seemed there was nothing sweeter to God than the sound of me praising His name on a Sunday morning.

Yes. Me!

> It is in the process of being worshipped that God communicates His presence to men.
> —C. S. Lewis

Because God didn't hear the screeching, the squawking, the pitchy voice, the bellowing, or any of the other horrendous sounds I'm more than capable of producing. He didn't plug His ears in horror, or protest the "melody" I was trying to make either. Nor did He whisper in my ear, or plead with my subconscious to *stop singing*. God was just elated I showed up—crooning His praises, lifting His name on high, and sending some love His way.

See, I've learned that vocalizing praise through song isn't about showcasing a gift or a talent (or the lack thereof in my case). Instead, it's about God. It's those minutes spent with Him in worship that are some of the most special; because no matter how hard my week has been, or what issues I'm facing, those moments of praise assist me in getting my heart and mind back in the place they need to be: appreciative, focused, and Christ-centered.

No matter how bad my melody is, the Lord makes it good. Maybe not Celine Dion kind of good, but "good" nonetheless.

He is my audience of One. So when it comes to worshipping God, sing it, sisters. Sing like you've never sung before. Embrace it each and every Sunday. Our Lord will never ask you to stop singing. Our God? He wants you to praise His name for all to hear. Sing and sing it loud.

> I will choose today to know my Savior, to be connected to Him, to love Him.
> —Lisa Chan

Breaking Bread (Communion)

As Jesus hung from that cross, His body beaten, mangled, and dying, He prayed to God. He called out: "My God, why have you forsaken me?" (Matt. 27:46). He begged for His Father to be near, when trouble was not far. That cry was soon followed by the most gut-wrenching words ever spoken, as Christ let out His last breath on this earth and proclaimed "It. Is. Finished" (John 19:30). After severe beatings, lashings, humiliation, and being nailed to a cross for His teachings, Jesus had succumbed to His wounds.

> For the message of the cross is foolishness to those who are perishing, but to us who are being saved it is the power of God.
> —1 Corinthians 1:18

He'd given up His spirit—He had paid the ultimate price . . . for us.

His mother wept; the disciples were frantic; anger and outrage were present as overwhelming sadness took over for the followers of the Messiah. But it was in those grief-laden moments, when the Son of God hung nailed to a cross, that the Almighty gave us the most unimaginable gift: salvation.

This is a gift to be remembered . . . it is a gift to be shared.

> We are told that as we approach the Lord's Table, *"Everyone ought to examine themselves before they eat of the bread and drink from the cup."*
> —1 Corinthians 11:28

Just as Christ broke bread and drank wine with His disciples during the Last Supper (prior to His crucifixion), we do so each week in church. We consume the "body" and "blood" of Christ in remembrance of His sacrifice. "And He took bread, gave thanks and broke it, and gave it to them, saying, 'This is my body given for you; do this in remembrance of me'" (Luke 22:19). Girls, this is how we honor Jesus. We pay tribute and offer gratitude . . . we remember by taking part in Communion.

Breaking bread? It's a pretty big deal. It's not something we do at church because we're supposed to, because it's a weekly ritual, or something we participate in because everyone else is doing it—God doesn't desire our half-hearted thanks or lackluster appreciation for such a gift. He desires our authenticity instead. His delight comes in hearing our gratitude. Because He sent His Son to die on that cross so that we could be reunited with Him when our life has come to pass, we must treat the Lord's Supper with reverence . . . for what and Whom it represents.

So each week—prior to consuming my little white cracker and cup of juice—I spend time in prayer with the Lord. I don't usually ask God for the things lying on my heart, nor do I place the emphasis of our conversation on myself. Instead, I just thank Him . . . for what He's given me, and for what Christ's death and eventual ascent into heaven mean to all of us.

I take a moment to reflect.

Because that "bread" isn't meant to be tossed into our mouths and washed down without any sort of reflection as to what these symbols represent. The body of Christ was bloodied and broken for us. He was killed for our transgressions. Communion is a covenant between us and our Savior—a pact, if you will—that we will attempt to live more like Him. It's my promise to do better and emote gratitude for His sacrifice . . . for His gift . . . for Him.

Breaking bread each and every week with fellow parishioners is so much more than just breaking bread.

It's remembering.

It's appreciation.

And it's love.

Moola (Tithes and Offerings)

Money is an interesting thing.

Each one of us needs it to survive, to buy the basic necessities for our lives, and yet, money can be the root of some serious evil as well. It's a weird relationship we have with currency and when it comes to giving it away, the same is true.

Especially when it comes to offering it to the church.

> *Each one must give as he has decided in his heart, not reluctantly or under compulsion, for God loves a cheerful giver.*
> **—2 Corinthians 9:7** ESV

Each year when Christmas and Easter rolled around (and after dressing up in my preteen finest), my family and I would head down to our local parish. I'd sit in a pew, listen to the words being spoken, the songs being sung, and spend most of the time fidgeting with my new threads. It was usually about halfway through mass, without fail, that a basket would be passed in front of each parishioner to collect money. I observed as this community of believers reached into their pockets, pulled out their wadded-up dollar bills, along with any spare change they could muster, and dropped it into the receptacle in front of them.

Person after person, row after row, they'd donate their money. And by the time it came for my family to do the same, the basket was usually full . . . overflowing with cash.

From the looks of it, it appeared the church was fairly wealthy. I saw twenty-dollar bills, and checks with lots of zeros on them. But no one ever told me *why* the money was being collected or what those funds were being used for. They simply waved that basket in front of us while everyone in proximity eyed the contributions being made.

Sitting there, I couldn't help but wonder why the church needed so much of the green stuff, and why our family *had* to contribute. I even questioned why my house of semiannual worship should receive any money at all, as I found myself half-tempted to pocket that currency rather than place it in the basket in front of me.

I can't believe I just admitted that.

But it's a question that many of us have, isn't it? Why the church keeps pressing us for our hard-earned money. A lot of people don't fully understand why we tithe, why we give financial offerings, or the importance in doing so.

The answer is simple: the church uses the money you provide to further its programs, its outreach, its missions work, and its service to the Lord. They use it to serve the city and love the people. And they use it to sustain their building, pay their staff, and run the church.

It's nothing new either, because this practice of tithing has been going on for centuries.

Dating back to Old Testament days, the Israelites were required to give 10 percent of their incomes back to God (Lev. 27:30–33). *Required!* There wasn't any question about it either—you gave a portion of your income and that was that. However, in the New Testament there's not one verse dictating how much a person needs to give to God, nor is there a predetermined percentage one should offer the church.

So why should we give?

Each man should give what he has decided in his heart to give, not reluctantly or under compulsion, for God loves a cheerful giver. (2 Cor. 9:7 NIV 1984)

You know, if you think about it, every good thing we receive comes from the Lord. This applies to our money as well. Even though we might've worked hard to earn those dollars, our circumstances and, ultimately, our wealth flow from Him. Our heavenly Father may not *need* our resources in order to accomplish His plans, but that's not to say He doesn't yearn to see us do good works with them . . . or to give back some of what He's blessed us with.

God calls us to tap into our hearts and pray about the monies we should offer our congregations. He asks that we give not out of a necessity or a commandment to do so, but a desire within. We are to give willingly, as we are able.

As he looked up, Jesus saw the rich putting their gifts into the temple treasury. He also saw a poor widow put in two very small copper coins. "I tell you the truth," he said, "this poor widow has put in more than all the others.

All these people gave their gifts out of their wealth; but she out of her poverty put in all she had to live on." (Luke 21:1–4 NIV 1984)

The money we make is meant to do so much more than sit in our bank accounts or buy the latest in gadgets, clothes, and material items. God has blessed us and in turn, shouldn't we bless others? Shouldn't we provide funding to the church and assist in furthering its ministries? Shouldn't we give back to God?

Because money doesn't have to be evil—not when it can be used for so much good.

Church under Fire

Sigh.

Make that a double sigh with a side of *umph.*

The bride of Christ—that's the name of the church, you know—sometimes gets herself into a bit of trouble, controversy, if you will. Yes. Sometimes the church, her pastors, and its various congregations can make mistakes, falter, and just plain mess up.

And the same goes for the people inside those churches, too.

Remember when I mentioned some of the issues you might've dealt with in the past? You know—others professing Christianity, saying one thing but doing another. Well, as much as I hate to say it, instances such as these can and do occur within church walls. Indeed, sometimes a house of worship and the people who frequent it can lose their way, their vision, the purpose of what they're there for and Who they're meant to serve.

Sometimes the bride of Christ can turn into a Bridezilla. And you know what? It ain't pretty.

Friends, this is the one topic I didn't want to touch with a ten-foot pole. Simply stated: I didn't want to write it. I'm uncomfortable discussing the stains, the blemishes, and the marks that some churches—and churchgoers alike—have placed on Christianity.

> *The church is a hospital for sick people, not a retirement home for the healthy.*
> —**Dr. Steven Crane**

I didn't want to admit that cases such as these exist, but I vowed to be honest, just as I promised to be real.

The church as a whole is under a lot of scrutiny these days. There are fingers being pointed and fighting underway. You've got one house of worship telling another that their thinking is wrong. While one church is preaching a certain doctrine, another is giving sermons on something completely different. You have mega churches attempting to appeal to the masses, while smaller churches feel they can't compete. You have nonbelievers questioning religious leaders—anxious to reveal heresy, false teachings, misconduct, and whatever else they can dig up.

The church has gotten a bad rap for sure. And you know what else? People are leaving. Some of those who grew up in the church no longer attend. Yep. Even with all of the information, teachings, and knowledge of the Word in their arsenal, our brothers and sisters are willingly choosing to leave the bride of Christ. Or pretend that she never existed at all.

But why?

A church can struggle for many reasons. But what's taking place today, and what people are finding is that some of us Christians are forfeiting our compassion, and losing sight of our hope. We're forgetting for Whom we exist, what He calls us to do—and Who we're supposed to serve. We're not loving people enough. We've grown too contented with our lives, consumed with ourselves, our needs . . . our wants.

Today, the majority of the unchurched population isn't interested in learning about God, just as they couldn't care less about knowing (or becoming) Christians. They've observed too many of us within the church and they don't like what they're seeing—our judging and condemning of others, and maintaining of our own selfish ways. They see us going about it all wrong, and they want no part in it.

Sigh.

> We need to stop giving people excuses not to believe in God. You've probably heard the expression "I believe in God, just not organized religion." I don't think people would say that if the church truly lived like we are called to live.
> —Francis Chan

Now, I'm not telling you this to discourage you, let alone keep you away from the church. Remember? I didn't even want to write this section in the first place. Rather, I'm sharing this information to help you understand that even though the majority of churches are teaching the gospel, preaching the Word of God, spreading love in every area they can possibly reach, there are others who have fallen away from this mission. Indeed, the church is an imperfect representation of a perfect God.

But our hearts are in the right place. The church does so much good. The majority of the people inside have the right motives. Many are doing God's work, witnessing to others. There are people who are unbelievably convicted and virtually on fire for the Lord and His Word. There are so many who are furthering the kingdom with their works and this is what I want to emphasize.

Believe me, girls, you are going to hear a lot about the church: people who dislike it, many who've walked away, others who won't even give it the time of day—but she's still the bride of Christ, made up of a family of believers—brothers and sisters in Christ united together by God. She's still the church and she exists for us, for our redemption and restoration. She exists for the world.

And she is loved.

Prescription for Praise

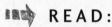 ## READ:

When Godly People Do Ungodly Things by Beth Moore
Called to Stay by Caleb Breakey
I Am a Church Member by Thom S. Rainer

STUDY:

Acts 20:28
Romans 12:3–5
1 Corinthians 10:31–33
1 Corinthians 12:12–26
Proverbs 3:9–10
Ephesians 1:18–23
Ephesians 5:25–32
Colossians 1:17–20
Colossians 3:14–16
1 Peter 2:9–10
Ephesians 2:10–22

▶ SING:

"If We are the Body" performed by Casting Crowns
"Let the Church Rise" performed by Jonathan Stockstill
"Jesus Loves the Church" performed by Phil Keaggy
"O Church, Arise" performed by Getty and Townend
"A New Hallelujah" performed by Michael W. Smith

▶ APPLY:

1. What are your thoughts about the church in general? Why do you think so many have stayed away?

_____

_____

2. Why is the church referred to as the bride of Christ?

_____

_____

3. Worshipping the Lord is about honoring God, giving gratitude and appreciation, coming together as a body, etc. What are your feelings concerning worship?

_____

_____

4. I mentioned that I'm a really bad singer. I also mentioned that God couldn't care less whether I sing like Celine Dion . . . or not. How do you feel about singing as it pertains to Sunday morning worship? Comfortable? Uncomfortable? Share your thoughts:

_____

_____

5. Have you had a bad experience at church? Has it prevented you from going back? Discuss the problems you encountered, the issues you faced. Lay them down right here. Get it all out.

_____

_____

_____

_____

_____

_____

_____

_____

_____

_____

_____

_____

_____

_____

_____

_____

_____

_____

_____

Never hold on to anything tighter than you're holding onto God.
—Jarrid Wilson

CHAPTER 7

Serving It Up

*I believe God wants us to love others so much
that we go to extremes to help them.*

—Francis Chan

We've all seen the commercials. A celebrity appears on-screen begging and pleading for you to send money to a third-world country. You see starving children living in deplorable conditions, impoverished and lacking clothing, schooling, medications, and the basic necessities that most North Americans take for granted. We watch, but more often than not, we as a collective society don't take the actions required in order to help, support, or serve the cause they're endorsing.

And we need to ask ourselves, *why*.

Why is the general population able to observe others in need, feel empathy and sadness for their plights, and yet still remain unwilling in their efforts to assist them? How are we able to witness such atrocities and do nothing—as if we hadn't been made aware, nor had any understanding of what's taking place halfway around the world, the nation, or even in our hometowns.

Maybe it's the hope that others will step up, you know— that another person (possibly with more money in his/her bank account) will aid these people. Yep—*someone else* will (probably) pick up that phone, offer financial support, and meet their needs. Someone else will serve.

But why not us?

> Most of us have enough knowledge and enough resources right now to change at least one person's life. It's not a matter of knowing there is a need. It is a matter of caring enough to do something about it. (Lisa Whittle)

For the first thirty years of my life, the whole idea of serving others was completely lost on me. I couldn't grasp the idea of such a thing, let alone understand why others would go out of their way to help another. I know that sounds harsh, and probably a bit difficult to comprehend (and believe me, it's even harder to admit), but it's no secret that I was wrapped up in myself, my issues, and my own wants and desires for a very long time. It wasn't that I didn't have a good heart or that I lacked compassion in general; I was just ignorant of the teachings of Christ . . . and was comfortable living a life that was, well, all about me.

You, my brothers and sisters, were called to be free. But do not use your freedom to indulge the flesh [sinful nature]; rather, serve one another humbly in love.
—Galatians 5:13

You see, serving others requires us to place ourselves second, third . . . or maybe even last. It means giving that first-place finish to another, putting someone else's needs above our own. It's complete selflessness on our parts.

As I look back, I now realize that I couldn't help but see the

world as it pertained to my own situation, *my* needs, and ultimately my desires for *my* life. And if I'm attempting to be truly
transparent here, I have to confess that those situations I saw on
TV—the ones that found others suffering from poverty, illness, and
a slew of other heart-wrenching issues—I prayed they would never
find *me*. I felt that if I could close my eyes and block out the noise
from a world that was pleading for my attention, those voices and
all of that suffering I'd turned a blind eye to would in fact go away.
I prayed for others' situations out of fear (you read that right)—fear
that one day those horrendous living conditions and diseases that
affected others might find me, too. That at any moment, another's
pain might become my own. That the comfortable life I'd known
(and felt secure in) would come to a screeching halt, all in a matter
of seconds.

Then what would I do?

What would I do if all I had left was to rely solely upon my
faith in Jesus and the people who love Him?

This sort of question, this type of thinking causes people to
open their eyes a bit. And for me, well, it forced me to dig deeper
and to start investing in someone other than myself. Today, when
I see those struggling to stay alive, starving for food, and plagued
by disease, the images affect me to my core. When I listen to the
testimonies and stories from missionaries who have devoted their
vacations (if not their lives) to assisting and ministering to others,
it makes me want to do more. To become better. It's in these
moments where the Holy Spirit convicts me. Where He pushes me
to say "yes" to serving those in need . . . where He reminds me to
die to myself and my selfish ways.

I now know, more than ever,
that rather than cozy up on my
couch and watch these people's

No one ever became
poor by giving.
—Anne Frank

predicaments unfold on the plasma screen in front of me, I need to take action instead.

I need to become the hands and feet of Jesus to someone else—someone in dire need of my love and attention. I need to get involved, and do my part, because God didn't create me to be a spectator. He didn't make me in His image for the sole purpose of living a comfortable existence—sidelined by my own security—out of the game and away from the action. Oh, friend, you and I were made for so much more than that—to do something instead of nothing, to serve others instead of ourselves.

The call to serve requires that we understand that the life we lead is not about us. It's about the One who first served us—up on that cross—and about the people He loves. It's about you and me meeting the needs of others, and loving people as Christ calls us to.

And it's refusing to do nothing.

Refusing to Do Nothing

> *I don't want to live like I don't care. I don't want to say another empty prayer.*
> —Josh Wilson,
> "I Refuse"

I once pondered the life and times of Jesus much differently than I do now. Since I never truly *knew* Him, never ran my fingers through the pages of a Bible, or practiced His teachings, I considered Jesus to be *just* another man. *Just* a person. I thought of His crucifixion as something that wasn't necessarily *for* me but an event that transpired—a historical incident that took place and was celebrated each year (with copious amounts of candy and one heinously large and slightly scary Easter Bunny). I never considered the death of the Messiah to be a gift, an act of love, let alone an act of service for *me*.

It took me (way) too long to realize and appreciate this one truth: Jesus Christ not only sacrificed His life for each one of us— His *life*, girls—but He's been serving us ever since.

This Jesus I speak of? He wasn't like most kings, was He? He didn't live among riches, nor did He wear the finest garments. He didn't dine with royalty either. Our Savior was born in a stable, of all places. Our Messiah? He sat with sinners, cared for the unlovable, cured the incurable, and served the unworthy . . . right up until His last breath.

The point I'm trying to make here, and what keeps popping into my mind, isn't why we *should* serve, the question is why *aren't* we serving more? Whether it's in our community, nation, or even abroad, our "job" is to share the message of Christ with others: those who are broken; those who are lost, scared, struggling, and hurting; those who are poor, impoverished, orphaned, widowed, and alone. Those who struggle just like we do.

> *For even the Son of Man did not come to be served, but to serve, and to give his life as a ransom for many.*
> **—Mark 10:45**

This is what love looks like. This is what Jesus did for the gentleman who couldn't see (John 9:1–11), for the man who couldn't walk (Mark 2:1–12), and for the leper no one would help (Mark 1:40–42). Jesus didn't look away. He didn't ignore them either. He embraced these people when no one else would and, more importantly, He loved them . . . unconditionally.

You and I are incapable of making the blind see. We can't make the lame walk, and we certainly can't cure a leper either. It's true. But we can make a difference in the lives of others . . . one person at a time. We can be the hands and feet of Jesus—spreading His joy, peace, and love as we're called to.

We can be so much more to so many.

God doesn't need your good works, your neighbor does.
—Martin Luther

TESTIMONY

Hands and Feet
Hester Christensen

Maybe you've heard the saying, "Be the hands and feet of Jesus." But what does this really mean? Jesus touched, healed, and cared for the practical needs of others. He entered the lives of those who were presumptuous and prideful and those who were downcast and destitute. His love and tenderness were evident. He saw past empty pockets, societal plagues, and cultural customs. Being the hands and feet of Jesus means letting others experience Christ, through our love of them that stems from our love of Him.

Serving is a big deal for a Christ follower because our purpose is to glorify Him and His kingdom, without considering what benefits us personally.

Being a biblical servant is really an attitude of the heart that removes self from the equation. Selfless people think less of themselves and more of the needs of others (Phil. 2:4). If we are selfless, we will serve with pure motives: to share Jesus. If we are selfish, we will serve with ulterior motives: to be recognized or rewarded.

Serving was Christ's demonstration of love to us. His example of humility beckons us to give up our lives for others, as an act of serving Him. But who exactly are "others"? They include our annoying neighbor, harsh boss, ungrateful in-laws, difficult friends, needy children, joy thieves, and anyone else who intersects our path.

This. Is. Hard. I get it. I'm guilty, too. The day-to-day demands and duties of our jobs, caring for a home and family, and all our other responsibilities easily wear us thin. It's especially hard to serve difficult people, but until we include ourselves in the category of undeserving, we will not fully realize the nature of our sin and how unworthy we are of Christ's love for us.

We can focus too easily on all we have to do instead of on the ministry God has given us. A shift to a more godly perspective teaches us that even routine things in life and familiar faces should be viewed as blessings, not burdens; as opportunities for ministry, not monotony. God gives us countless opportunities to serve each day: our families, co-workers, spouses, children, neighbors . . .

Regardless of our jobs, positions, or influence . . . Christians are called to serve like Christ.

It is vital to our spiritual health that we invest what is entrusted to us to advance the Kingdom; that we serve, not expect to be served. Our humble servant, Jesus, did not serve to be applauded or rewarded; neither should His people.

This reminds me of a time when I was exceedingly selfish and too focused on the temporal.

After spending twelve hours downtown rubbing shoulders with two hundred fifty thousand people at the world's largest basketball 3-on-3 tournament, walking numerous miles to and from our boys' games, and sitting in the scorching sun, I was ready to crawl into a hole for a week. Unfortunately, my boys won their games and advanced (you can stop laughing now). So I knew I needed rest to prepare for more mayhem in the city the following morning.

We arrived home at 8:15 p.m., emptied the cooler, and threw the boys in the shower and then bed. I had just slipped into my happy clothes, a.k.a., my jammies. Yes! I wanted nothing more than to study the back of my eyelids.

All I wanted was sleep. All I needed was a bit of shut-eye. All I craved were hours of unconscious darkness. But what I needed was a spiritual spanking.

"Guess who is here?" my husband snickered. I was in no mood for jokes.

"What do you mean, who's here?" I retorted. A quick look out the front window sent my exhausted flesh into a frenzy! My anger rating went from 0 to 212 in about 3 seconds flat!

"What is he doing here? It's 8:45 and I do not have the energy to visit! How come he never calls? It's late, honey, and we don't get to sleep in tomorrow! This is crazy! I cannot do this!"

My husband was tired, too, but he graciously opened the door to our unexpected guest while I marched down the hall to pray with our boys (not that my attitude was right for that either).

I made my way back to the kitchen, faked a pleasant greeting to our visitor, and went about packing lunches for the next day of the tournament.

While my husband and unwanted guest chatted at the dining table, the Lord spoke to my heart, "You haven't even offered him a cup of water."

I reluctantly extended a full glass and went back to work.

Again the Lord spoke, "You should ask him if he's eaten dinner."

Dinner?! What?! But, Lord, it's nine o'clock and I just want to go to bed. I mean, I've been gone all day. Can't I take care of myself and just collapse into bed? You know how much I need my sleep. People don't just "pop in" for dinner and a visit at 9 P.M., you know.

Arguing with God is futile.

Our guest hadn't eaten since lunch. When I offered a sandwich, he ordered it with the works. I began to assemble the eight-layer tower, chopping with extra fierceness, nearly abusing the vegetables for the inconvenience this man was causing me.

After delivering my leaning tower of selfishness—I mean sandwich masterpiece—to our guest, I went into our bathroom. Finally, I was in a place of solace and peace, or so I thought.

While washing up, I noticed toothpaste all over my brand-new hand towel a girlfriend had recently given me. I was already torqued and this just lit me up!

Eerrrggh! Why can't our boys keep the toothpaste in their mouths? Why do they have to wipe their oozing mouths all over my nice towel?!

In this moment the Holy Spirit spoke profoundly to my tired, anxious, irritated heart: "You're way too concerned with having a clean towel, Hester. Truth is, your towel isn't dirty enough. To be my servant, you need a dirty towel."

Ouch.

The Lord's conviction broke the dam. Where a previously tight-lipped scowling face existed, there was now a countenance washed with the waters of repentance. *Indeed, Lord, dirty towels are your tools for serving.*

I missed a divine appointment to minister to someone who needed to be loved through service. Even though I superficially served a sandwich, God supernaturally changed my heart.

My mind recalled John 13. The account of Jesus washing His disciples' feet is tender. Our Lord and King humbled Himself to serve His men by taking the lowliest position: "So he got up from the meal, took off his outer clothing, and wrapped a towel around his waist. After that, he poured water into a basin and began to wash his disciples' feet, drying them with the towel that was wrapped around him" (John 13:4–5).

In the first century, foot washing was a task given to servants as an act of hospitality to guests. Maybe the servant of this home was gone or the disciples just skipped over the traditional customs of washing. Jesus stepped up to serve by kneeling to wash. He used this moment to teach His inner circle of followers. His example communicated a critical truth for those who were to follow Him, by showing exactly how they were to minister to others by taking the position of a servant.

In John 13:14–15, Jesus says, "Now that I, your Lord and Teacher, have washed your feet, you also should wash one another's feet. I have set you an example that you should do as I have done for you." This is one of

Christ's parting exhortations before His crucifixion just hours later. Our love of God is materialized when we love others.

In effect, servants of Christ are to give up their lives for the will of Christ in order to advance His kingdom. We are to minister to others by being devoted to serve their interests above our own, even when it may be inconvenient.

Foot washing may not be customary today, but regardless, opportunities for serving abound. Within our homes, communities, schools, and churches, there are people who need to connect and experience the love of Christ through us—His hands and feet.

There's no disclaimer in Christ's teaching. He doesn't say, "Only the kindhearted, middle class, educated . . . only those with the right personality and temperament can serve." Nope. Every person who follows Christ is called to be a servant.

I'll repeat again: This. Is. Not. Easy. There are times when we just don't feel like serving others. When our physical strength appears limited or when people are ungrateful, let's remember the towel.

- Dirty towels are Christ's tools for ministry.
- Dirty towels are His measure of biblical greatness.

God measures greatness by smallness. Christ desires for His followers to do as He did for us, by serving others in His name. Is your towel sanitary? Stained? Spotless? Soiled? How dirty is your towel?

Called to Serve

You are now entering the mission field.

I see it every time I leave church. Every Sunday as I pull out of the parking lot, I read the sign inscribed with this message—and it's a reminder . . . a dose of reality. The city I live in, the people I meet, and the entire world around me represent the mission field:

the people I'm called to serve, love, and witness to.

It's helping a friend out when her child is sick.

It's reaching out to the widow who feels alone.

It's making a meal for the family who just lost a loved one.

> *Open your eyes to the mission field in front of you. Witness, disciple, and love others . . . in Christ's name.*
> —**Jenny Lee Sulpizio**

It's sending a care package halfway around the world to a soldier who's homesick.

It's reaching out to a population of nonbelievers who have yet to open a Bible, read the teachings of Christ, or hear of God's promises.

It's all these things and so much more.

But I'd like to stop right here for a minute. I'd like to check in and see how you're doing. I know this might seem like an awkward pause and all, but I think it's necessary. See, for far too long, I felt ashamed for not helping out enough. For sitting at home while watching others step up and serve . . . for watching my neighbors assist, lead, and love. I harbored feelings of guilt for not attempting to be more like Jesus sooner, for not doing my part. But the whole point in my writing this chapter isn't to make *you* feel that way.

Not in the least.

Friends, there have been way too many times in my walk where I've mistaken guilt for conviction. Plenty of times where I let that shame control me, too. But, here's what you need to know: conviction comes from the Holy Spirit, who

> *For while we make a living by what we get, we make a life by what we give.*
> —**Ronald Reagan**

softens the hardness in my heart, channels my empathy and my compassion, and then calls me to action.

However, guilt? That's not born of the heavens. That's not something from God. Those feelings of remorse that tend to rise up within are fueled by the Enemy, and I have to warn you not to confuse the two.

> *Guilt immobilizes you. Conviction leads you to change . . . to action.*
> **—Paul Mondragon**

Because it's so easy to do.

You are now aware of what it means to serve. You understand the importance of helping someone other than yourself, why you should provide assistance, and that in doing so, you are in fact accomplishing God's work here on earth.

And finally, serving is not a competition. Providing an act of service isn't about what others see. It's not about recognition, or how much money one can donate to a certain cause. It's about a real desire, a genuine itch to help people, to do more. Girls, the Lord's not keeping a scorecard in heaven because our works won't buy our way there. But it's in those God-given gifts He's provided us with that we're being called to action. And that's what makes the body of Christ so remarkable . . . all of our talents, carved out from the beginning, used to glorify God, together, in unity.

> *By this everyone will know that you are my disciples, if you love one another.*
> **—John 13:35**

When it comes to serving, God's not asking us to one-up each other, the Lord's not asking you to volunteer your time in order to extinguish those feelings of guilt and shame either. Nope. He's asking for your heart to be in it. He's asking for you.

Serve, girls, because He first served us.

God's definition of what matters is pretty straightforward. He measures our lives by how we love.
—Francis Chan

Prescription for Praise

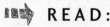 **READ:**

Serve Strong by Terry Powell

Kisses from Katie by Katie Davis

7: An Experimental Mutiny against Excess by Jen Hatmaker

Live to Make a Difference by Max Lucado

Barefoot Church by Brandon Hatmaker

The Irresistible Revolution by Shane Claiborne

Interrupted by Jen Hatmaker

Giving and Tithing by Larry Burkett

Rhinestone Jesus by Kristen Welch

 **STUDY:**

Matthew 20:26

John 12:26

Hebrews 6:10

Romans 12:10–11

Romans 12:4–7

Colossians 3:23–24

 **SING:**

"I Refuse" performed by Josh Wilson

"Hands and Feet" performed by Audio Adrenaline

"Live with Abandon" performed by Newsboys

"Let Them See You" performed by Colton Dixon

APPLY:

1. What's one misconception you've had about serving others?

_____

_____

2. Has this chapter changed your thoughts on serving in general? Why or why not?

_____

_____

3. When discussing acts of service, I mentioned "dying to one's self." What do you think I meant by this?

_____

_____

4. How can you show love to others? What simple acts in your community can you participate in? Share some ideas here.

_____

_____

5. Serving others isn't about guilt or shame. As we just discussed, God doesn't want us to serve because we think we *should*, but out of the desire to show the love of Christ toward another. Thoughts?

_____

_____

*I prefer a church which is bruised, hurting and dirty
because it has been out on the streets,
rather than a church which is unhealthy from being
confined and from clinging to its own security.*
—Pope Francis

CHAPTER 8

Me against the World

Our society strives to avoid the possibility
of offending anyone—except for God.

—Billy Graham

I *used* to think we lived in a wonderful world.

No, really.

Before becoming a Christian, I used to look at this place around me and be able to hum along to that famous tune by Louis Armstrong (the "wonderful world" one) . . . and mean it. It was easy to see beauty in my surroundings: the environment in which I lived, the amazing settings that nature provided, and even the goodwill of human beings toward one another. I loved everything about this world—the people, the places, and all the "things" in it. But over the past few years, I'll admit my views have changed, my outlook has darkened, and I guess you could say I'm struggling to try and figure this place out.

Believe me, I know how that sounds. I get the pessimism and lack of encouragement I just relayed. I understand it's not a very Christian attitude to have either. But hear me out for a second . . . hear what I have to say.

See, I've got to be honest about what I'm feeling and seeing, and how the behaviors I've observed around me have opened my eyes in ways I wish they hadn't.

The same world I *used* to love living in has become a place that at times rejects, persecutes, and mocks me for my spiritual beliefs. It's a place that for the most part refuses to know Christ, let alone practice the teachings of the Bible. It's a world that has decidedly pushed God away, rejected His Word, His ways, His laws . . .and even His love.

And I don't know why.

> *Do not love this world nor the things it offers you, for when you love the world, you do not have the love of the Father in you.*
> **—1 John 2:15** NLT

It appears that making the decision to live according to God's Word and professing a belief in Jesus Christ, by our culture's standards is a pretty unpopular move these days. In fact, the very society who once feared the Lord, who once revered Him as the all-powerful, the Almighty, the Great I Am, has collectively discounted His very being. Instead, we've morphed into a people more concerned with creating our own laws than we are with adhering to the ones divinely set in place. We've evolved into a culture that balks at the mere mention of God, one that finds ourselves enraged by His interruptions into our daily lives. I hate to say it, but we are a place, a people, a world that's become . . . *lost.*

Now, I understand that these are some pretty heavy statements to make. Bold even. And, of course, I'm generalizing here because not everyone feels this way . . . nor do they act in this manner. But too many of us do. Too many of us have forgotten about Jesus. We've ignored His sacrifice, overlooked His grace, and scoffed at His promises. In this upside down world, we've willingly made God an outsider.

But that's just it: God hasn't changed, friends.

We have.

Look around. Whether it's the government, the schools, our towns, or our population as a whole, it's evident from the current state of our world that Jesus doesn't fit in.

> When you realize life is war, you make prayer a shield and Christ your general and the victory is found in grace.
> —Ann Voskamp

And for those of us who follow Him, it appears we don't either.

It pains me to say that—to describe God and His Son as outsiders to the very people they saved, but it's true. Girls, the purpose of our lives isn't to win some popularity contest. It's not about our social status; how many friends we have on Facebook, or the number of followers on our Twitter accounts. Rather, our purpose is to do God's work, love others, uphold His Word, and glorify Him. Our objective is to fit in with God's plan for our lives, not cater to what the world around us dictates we should be or ought to believe.

We're not here to blend into our surroundings . . . we're here to stand up and stand out for God. We're here to be bold for Jesus.

> The greatest prison people live in is the fear of what other people think.
> —Unknown

Fitting In

Remember those years spent in high school? After reading this question, you probably just did one of two things: thought back upon those times with fondness; or distorted your face, furrowed your brow, and sighed in relief—thankful those tumultuous years are a thing of the past. For most of us (my hand's raised high on this one), high school represented a time when we girls yearned to fit in. I mean, none of us *wanted* to feel like outcasts, right? No, we wanted a niche, a safe place, and the security that comes from feeling like we belong.

Hey, those days of teenage angst may be a thing of the past (thank goodness!), but that longing to fit in never really goes away. Those feelings are still present—that desire is still there. I sense it too, but when it comes to measuring up to society's standards, I've finally accepted the fact that I don't belong . . . and it's okay. The Bible says we're sojourners and strangers to this world, and that fitting in and gaining others' approval is not our goal. It's not why we were put on this earth.

It's who we are in the eyes of God that's of utmost importance, and it's our identity in Him where we'll find that safety and security . . . the place where we truly belong.

> *The further a society drifts from the truth, the more it will hate those that speak it.*
> —**George Orwell**

When it comes to professing Christianity and claiming to be God's girl, your interactions with others may not always be pleasant. Unfortunately, you may get some strange looks (speaking from experience, of course). Some may laugh at you. Others may roll their eyes and mock your beliefs. Your friends may distance themselves and your relatives may think you've lost your mind. If your immediate circle has yet to know Christ, it's quite possible they won't grasp your hunger to. They won't get where you're coming from, and oftentimes people denounce what they don't understand—what they fear.

But take heart. Once you've awakened to how life *should* be lived—once you recognize the significance in having a relationship with God and His Son—the world's views cease to matter. So be strong, friend, and know that the weight of this world might feel overwhelming at times, but the peace and love God guarantees, the strength and comfort He promises, and the future we're set to inherit for such a devotion are so worth it. Why settle for fitting in to your surroundings when you were made to stand out for Him?

Please hear my heart: the world in its entirety is *not* a bad place. God created it, after all. But as a people, we've strayed. We've wandered from the teachings of Christ. We've forgotten about God. So when it comes to connecting with your heavenly Father, it may not be the "in" thing to do, but the salvation we're seeking is much too important to worry about such trivial things. Girls—you weren't placed on this earth to impress its residents, nor are you living for their approval. Our focus should be to shine the light on God, not ourselves.

So let others think what they want, allow them to poke fun, make comments, and the like. Persecution for such beliefs is a given these days. Indeed, it's bound to happen. But through it all, set your sights on Him by refusing to fit in . . . well, at least on this side of heaven, that is.

Remember, the glory we seek is not our own. It's for God and God alone.

Identity Crisis

Ignoring that itch to belong is easier said than done. It's simple to say you won't conform to the ideas and opinions of this culture, or care about what others think—but let's get real: I alone have spent a good portion of my life trying to fit into a certain mold . . .

to be popular, well liked, and known. That desire to click with others is normal. And when it comes to ditching the ways of this world, well, let's just say it doesn't happen overnight.

> The more you seek Jesus, the less you'll seek approval from the world.
> —Jarrid Wilson

Finding our true identities starts with taking a serious look within, focusing on how we live, what our priorities are, where our hearts lie, and what we deem most important. It means examining our relationships, our dialogue, as well as the way we treat and interact with others. It's taking these lives of ours and placing them under a microscope.

And sometimes, that can be scary.

When we're forced to look inward—when we run a self-diagnostic—we don't always like what we see, who we are, or what we've become. But it's a starting point, right? It's where change can begin, and where our thinking can transform. It's in these moments where our lives can start over, fresh in Christ, where we can begin seeing this world through a completely different lens.

> It is better to have God approve, than the world applaud.
> —Thomas Watson

Mark 10:17–22 recalls the biblical account of the rich young ruler looking to achieve eternal life. Jesus informs the young man that in order to follow Him, he'll need to cast aside all of his worldly possessions. All of his "stuff." As you could imagine, the man was taken aback—confused by Jesus' request. Get rid of all of his things? All of the items he had worked so hard for, in order to follow Jesus? How could anyone obey such a command? How could anyone be expected to forfeit such a stash? Saddened by this request, the man left with his items still in tow. But he left without Jesus.

Poor guy. Didn't he get it? Didn't he understand how temporary all those possessions were? I mean, he chose his worldly belongings over the Son of God. Over Jesus. He opted for "stuff" instead of salvation.

Crazy, right?

By today's standards, I'm willing to bet that a number of us might do the same thing. I'm thinking that only a small percentage of the current North American population would be willing to chuck it all: the cars, the house, the nice clothes, and the expensive jewelry in order to follow the Son of God.

But the question is *why*?

Too many of us (generally speaking) have become so focused on the bright and shiny objects of this world that not even God in the

> *Stuff doesn't fill emptiness. It just hides it.*
> —**Kristen Welch**

flesh could sway us from our distractions. It's as if our identities can be found in the objects we own, and the items we hope to one day attain, rather than the One who gave us everything. The same One who breathed life into our bodies (Gen. 2:7) and wishes to dwell within our hearts is the very One we've chosen to ignore, to replace.

Ouch.

Friends, stepping into Christianity—into a life with Christ—means so much more than anything we could ever own, purchase, or obtain. The material possessions we desire, the wealth we long to have? They're worth nothing. When it comes to our eternity, all of this "stuff" is just so . . . temporary.

Maybe we should stop looking around at what others are doing, saying, and wearing. Maybe we should make a conscience effort to stop being so consumed with what other people have and what this world can provide. You and me? Let's focus on Christ instead, on what His Word says, and what His teachings show.

> *To receive our true identity from Jesus we must first let go of the false identities we hold.*
> —**David Lomas**

Once again, our identities can't be found in things we own, or the riches we possess. Our true identity is who we are in Christ.

Believe that. Know it. Hold it as truth.

You were made by God and for God—and until you understand that, life will never make sense.
—**Rick Warren**

False Idols

> *We never become who God created us to be by trying to be like everybody else.*
> —**Tim Tebow**

I *used* to watch the Oscars.

In fact, I can vividly remember when I was a young girl looking forward to this annual evening in Hollywood where famous movie stars would congregate together. I'd watch as beautiful actresses made their way down the red carpet decked out in gorgeous (not to mention incredibly expensive) gowns, the finest jewels, and oh-so-glamorous attire. I observed as others took in their beauty, treated them like royalty, and would seemingly do anything just to get next to them. As an impressionable young thing, these women represented everything I wanted to be as an adult: beautiful, successful, loved . . . and perfect.

I idolized everything about them.

But what I failed to realize at the time was that those women who took to that stage, the same ladies who sauntered down those aisles and claimed their awards, they were just people. Sure, they were women who had a talent—who had worked hard for the privileges afforded to them in their lives—but all in all, they were still just people. The problem? I was treating them like they were something more. I mean, why was I so transfixed by their public personas anyways? Why did I hope to one day possess the same things? Why was I so in awe of these women, but couldn't have cared less about Jesus?

Celebrities make movies. They sing songs. They appear on television shows.

But Jesus? He sacrificed His life for *our* eternal salvation.

Friends, we've been doing this all wrong.

Too often we place our focus on the creations rather than the Creator. Especially as females, it seems like we always want what we don't have. We get hung up on it, start finding fault with our bodies, our hair, our appearance, and our lives. When we look to the surface rather than looking inward, false idols breed and insecurities run rampant.

It's how we get hung up . . . it's how our reality gets distorted.

But here's what I know to be true: whether you're rich or poor, have nice things or nothing at all, look like a model or quite the oppo-

> *Those who pay regard to vain idols forsake their hope of steadfast love.*
> **—Jonah 2:8** ESV

site, we are all human, and we all stand before Jesus the same way when our time here ends.

Today, it's rare that I catch one of these award shows, and when I do, I find nothing glamorous about them. Instead, I see a number of women struggling under the pressures their industry has placed on them. I see a collective group of people who appear to be wrapped up in external beauty, riches, and the temporary things of this world . . . and it's in complete opposition to everything I know and am learning about Christ.

I'll admit: A lot of what I've seen in our culture has brainwashed my thinking. It has led me to believe that I actually *need* more money, more clothes, more things . . . more. But this isn't the truth. This isn't what the Bible states. God's not asking me to store up earthly treasures (Matt. 6:19–21). He's not telling me that the person with the most stuff wins either. So why is our world telling us this?

I feel like I've been duped. Like I've been fed a load of lies. And in many ways I have.

It's biblical truth that we need to place our trust in, girls—not the false idols of this world. It's the truth—the Word of God—that will indeed set us free.

TESTIMONY

Telling Yourself the Truth
Laura S. Cabanillas

It was our first meeting. She wasn't even thirty years old, and she felt her life was over. "I hate my life. I hate myself. I'm a failure. Nothing I do is good enough. I mess up everything." With tears streaming down her cheeks, she lamented for several minutes, citing every negative message that cycled through her head, every moment of every day. Finally, worn out from her own inner chatter, she lay her head back on the leather couch, closed her eyes, and let out a deep sigh, "I can't do this anymore."

"Good," I offered. "I want you to try something different." Her eyes remained shut. I waited. Silence filled the room. I needed her to be interested. She had to be willing. I couldn't do it for her. As we sat in silence, I began to pray that hope would fill her heart. After several minutes, slowly, like a drawbridge being raised, she lifted her head and revealed eyes hollow from exhaustion.

"You've got to start telling yourself the truth," I began gently. "All of these things you say to yourself relentlessly are wearing you down. Your negative self-talk is sucking the life right out of you."

"I don't know what the truth is, other than this," she threw her hand up in a gesture of surrender. "I'm just repeating what everyone else tells me: my husband, my boss, my parents. If everyone else thinks I'm a failure, I guess it must be true."

"You're listening to the wrong voices," I almost whispered. "There is someone else whose voice outweighs them all on what's really true about you."

I stopped purposely and paused to see if she was interested. Eyes narrowing inquisitively, she tilted her head and sat up a little straighter. "Go on."

I did. And we did—go on and keep meeting, that is. For several months, we worked together regularly and this particular client blossomed into a bright-eyed, optimistic young lady filled with hope for the future. Not that any one thing in her life changed drastically. But one person did. She did. She started telling herself the truth. Every moment of every day. And it made all the difference.

I work with women every day who find themselves stuck in a cycle of toxic thinking. They construct faulty core beliefs about themselves and the world around them, based on years of listening to negative messages and half-truths by both the media and people in their sphere of influence. We all have people in our lives who say hurtful things, whose words we believe for one reason or another; maybe they are someone we like, or even love. Maybe they are an authority figure, someone we respect. But as all people are imperfect, lots of imperfect things come out of our mouths, and those words create something. Like seeds scattered in a garden, words take root in our minds. The destructive messages are weeds that run rampant, and choke out the life-giving messages of truth.

With so many voices around us competing for a plot in the garden of our minds—family, friends, co-workers, media, culture—it can be confusing and draining to try to figure out what messages are true, or even helpful. Enter the Master Gardener.

No one knows us better than the One who created us. God created us to live meaningful lives filled with peace, love, hope, faith, grace, and joy. We lose those things when we start believing all of the lies planted in our heads that take root through the many influences around us, instead of believing the truth. Romans 12:2 tells us that we can "be transformed by the renewing of [our] mind[s]." That's what happened to the client I mentioned above. Once she weeded her garden of all her stinkin' thinkin', she began to feel much better about herself. I saw a visible change in her, as she began to listen to what God says about her, rather than what everyone else says.

It's actually a very simple process. You begin by writing down every negative, unhelpful, self-destructive thought you have. If you aren't sure if a thought falls into that category, ask someone you trust to help you decide. Then, write a truthful counter statement for every faulty one: something that is positive, helpful, and affirming. If you feel you don't know what's true, you can always find the truth in the Bible. God's Word is filled with true and powerful messages you can use to plant seeds of life. Listen to Him by going to His Word. Start telling yourself the truth. You will find that you begin to have more grace for yourself, and others.

If you're skeptical about how telling yourself the truth can bring more grace into your life, try an experiment: After you write down a list of positive, truthful, affirming statements, try saying them aloud, while looking at yourself in the mirror, every day for thirty days. Listen to your voice speak life and truth every day. Notice if your mood improves, if your attitude becomes more hopeful, if your choices take a turn toward the positive. Notice if it becomes easier to decipher the voice of life from the voice of lies. Notice there is only a one-letter difference between life and lie . . . sometimes it's that subtle in the messages that clamor for our attention.

Listen closely. Speak confidently.

You are loved. Let that be the first statement on your list. Go on . . . tell yourself the truth.

On His Side

Before moving on, I feel the need to further explain this chapter. See, this portion of the book wasn't meant to serve as a place where I preach, hold firm to my soapbox, or allow my opinions to run rampant. I don't want to project negativity about our immediate surroundings or the ones we love either. Instead, I needed to share what's on my heart. I needed to explain what I've seen and what I've dealt with in my experiences thus far. The world around us can be a tough place to live, hard to navigate, and, as Christians—as those who choose to follow Christ—there are going to be times when we'll face rejection. A lot of it. Whether it's from friends, family members, or even from a random person we've never even met before. People are going to have opinions—some of which will be in complete aversion to Christian beliefs. Others will express their contempt for Jesus, and their hatred toward God. But in this oftentimes dark world, you can be the light. You can shine for Him.

Even though it may not be deemed popular within our culture, I have to tell you: it's okay to side with Jesus.

It's okay to throw up your hands to the images seen on TV, as well as the stories told in the media. It's all right to survey your surroundings and feel as though something's just not right, not adding up. It's perfectly fine if your beliefs differ from trendy worldviews.

Jesus is telling you, *it's okay.*

Growing in your Christian faith, praising the Lord, spreading the love of Christ, and finding your identity in Him is what matters.

It's what's most important.

I have come as a light to shine in this dark world, so that all who put their trust in me will no longer remain in the dark.
—John 12:46 NLT

Prescription for Praise

 READ:

Restless by Jennie Allen
Radical by David Platt
Love Idol by Jennifer Dukes Lee
Crash the Chatterbox by Steven Furtick
Gods at War by Kyle Idleman

 STUDY:

Exodus 20:3–4
Colossians 3:5–6
Jeremiah 2:5
1 Samuel 12:21
Matthew 19:23–24
Luke 6:24–25
Mark 10:21–25
1 Timothy 2:1–10

SING:

"Me Without You" performed by TobyMac
"My Own Little World" performed by Matthew West
"The Motions" performed by Matthew West
"This Man" performed by Jeremy Camp
"There Will Be a Day" performed by Jeremy Camp

"It's Your Life" performed by Francesca Battistelli
"You Are for Me" performed by Kari Jobe

APPLY:

1. Do you find yourself getting caught up in the things of this world? It's easy to do, isn't it? How can you keep your sights set above instead of focused on your surroundings?

_____

_____

2. Read 1 Timothy 2:1–10. What is this passage saying to you? Explain what Paul is telling believers.

_____

_____

3. Think about your immediate circle of friends and family. What would they think about you entertaining Christianity? Would they support you in pursuing Christ? Ponder this for a moment. Would you be embarrassed to share Jesus with them? Be honest. It's okay.

_____

_____

4. At this point in your walk, do you find yourself struggling in your attempts to fit in? Share your thoughts now.

_____

_____

5. What about idolatry? False idols? Do you find yourself placing other people, possessions, and material items before God? If so, how can this change?

_____

_____

And let the peace that comes from Christ rule in your hearts. For as members of one body you are called to live in peace. And always be thankful.
—Colossians 3:15 NLT

CHAPTER 9

Relationship vs. Religion

Religion is learning about love.
Relationship is about living loved.

—Ann Voskamp

Authentic. Genuine. Real. True. Deep.

As I think about the relationship I want with Christ, as well as the type of devotion I hope to emote toward my heavenly Father, these five words come to mind. See, I'm not interested in religious rituals, wearing my Sunday best accessorized with a plastic smile, or a superficial connection with the bride of Christ. Nor am I all that concerned with becoming a well-versed Christian capable of rattling off countless verses of Scripture, but unable to engage with the One who wrote them.

Entering a personal relationship with our Savior isn't about going through the motions. It's not about looking the part, or acting a certain way either. It's about getting real.

What I'm trying to say here is that our desire should be to pursue, recognize, and know our Lord as well as He already knows us (Jer. 1:5). We need to roll up our sleeves and get to work on our faith, routinely set our eyes on the Word, and participate in a meaningful union with our Creator. Personally, I want to live for Him, just as I want others to see Him living in me. I want unshakeable faith—the kind of love and devotion that's contagious to others. I want to reflect His light—so that others may see and want to do the same.

But a relationship such as this takes work, right? In fact, every connection we've made in our lives thus far (whether it's with a spouse, family member, or friend) takes effort. A lot of it. And those relationships we form tend to be the center of our lives— they're what we hold most dear.

So shouldn't it be the same way when it comes to our Savior? Shouldn't the relationship we have with the living God be our first concern? Our top priority? Perhaps placed above all others?

Shouldn't God come first?

> *God wants full custody of His children, not just weekend visits.*
> **—Tony Evans**

Hey, our Lord wants all of us—our whole heart, our complete attention, and our unwavering gratitude. But what happens when our attempts fall short? When we feel distant from and don't know how to talk to Him? What happens when it is a struggle to obtain the relationship we desire to have with God?

This spiritual journey we're pursuing begins by actively seeking Him and His Word. It's in prayer. It's attending church, connecting with our brothers and sisters in Christ, and it's making the decision to accept Him. It's taking that first step and marching into His presence.

But you know what? It seems like all too often we find other things to fill our time and sway our attention. Generally speaking, our attempts at forming an authentic relationship with our Creator have, indeed, become distracted.

Time to Refocus

Gosh—it must've been about five or six years ago now that I settled in one evening to watch the latest Disney film with my three children. The popcorn was popped, the blankets were out, and the Kleenex was handy. Without fail—and just ten

> *You will look for Me and find Me, when you look for Me with all your heart.*
> **—Jeremiah 29:13** NLV

minutes into viewing said film—this sweet flick had me blubbering like an idiot and crying the "ugly cry." The message of the movie began tugging those heartstrings of mine as I sat in the middle of my living room, surrounded by my children and one huge bucket of popcorn.

It forced me to pause and focus on the blessings curled up in my lap, resting on my arm, sharing my snack, and calling me "Mom." And as the film broached the topic of true purpose in our lives, it left me mulling over the deeper meaning of my own.

All of that in just ten minutes of viewing time, folks!

However, those moments of reflection and gratitude were short-lived. Yep, in an instant, those emotions I'd acknowledged got pushed aside as I continued to stuff my face with food and reengage with the plot of the movie.

And it was in the character of a little dog named Dug where I found familiarity. Don't laugh. I watched as this mutt played out on screen what I myself portrayed in real life. There he was, maniacally searching for what he thought would bring the recognition and love he desperately craved. There he was wanting and wishing to be liked, loved, and appreciated for who he was, yet his attempts were futile. As he searched and searched for something to make him complete, the one thing on this earth that would earn his approval, he became distracted. So much so that in the moment a loving master walked in, he was unable to recognize it. What he desired was standing right there in front of him, and yet he was too distracted by the task at hand to truly appreciate such a blessing.

Despite his best intentions, Dug couldn't help but get caught up in his surroundings, distracted by a silly little squirrel of all things (referring to the movie *Up*, of course).

And as my bucket of popcorn dwindled down, as my children nodded off to sleep, I was left pondering this message. And that's when it hit me: my distractions (the squirrels in my life, so to speak) had my full attention. I'd been looking to the left and right, so caught up in the chaos of my life that it never really occurred to me to look up and in. I was failing to understand that the distance I felt toward God was present because I had put it there. That gap was my own doing. That void was because of me.

I. Was. Distracted.

We need to make peace with who we are so insecurities don't become a distraction to how we live.
—Lysa Terkeurst

And you know what? It's happening to us all.

In this day and age, we're too busy. There's so much going on in our lives that we're becoming consumed by it, devoured, you could say. Our relationship with Christ is taking a backseat to our chaos, and this connection—this bond we're trying to form—is getting lost along the way. We're allowing other things to invade our time.

The "squirrels" are infiltrating, friends, and we're missing out (big time) because of it.

I mean, what if we were more interested in God? Let's think about this for a minute: What if we could be easily distracted by Him instead of the things of this world? What if we could forget about the craziness of our schedules for a minute and place our focus on Him?

Forming a genuine relationship with the Lord means living complete, whole, and with the confidence that nothing on this earth could ever take away or threaten to destroy the love He has for you. Ever. Nothing you can do can make Him love you less . . . or more. Nothing can separate us . . . except for our own selves and those pesky distractions standing in our way.

Growing Up

You know, I once read that a healthy relationship encourages growth. This makes perfect sense, actually. Relationships of all kinds cause us to grow in one way or another, stretch our minds, expand our thinking, open our hearts, and

> *Coming out of the dark, I finally see the light now and it's shining on me.*
> —**Gloria Estefan**

so forth. But when we're talking about God, relationship is one thing—organized religion is another, eh?

There seems to be a lot of confusion when it comes to relationship with God and the religion we practice. I think many of us have varying ideas as to what it means and, better yet, what religion's really like.

As a woman who spent a lot of time observing Christianity from the outside, I couldn't help but find myself turned off by the religion of it all. Seriously. Whether it was the Ten Commandments describing the list of things *I shall not* do, or the perception I had of what a Christian *should* look and act like, I was skeptical. The relationship with my Creator is what I craved—but the religion of it all is what I feared.

> *Jesus didn't come to start a religion. He came to have a relationship with you. He has a purpose and destiny for your life.*
> **—Unknown**

And this was a dangerous place to dwell.

After eight years into this journey with Christ, I'm keenly aware of just how much seeking a relationship with God—Christ as well as the Holy Spirit—and religion go hand in hand. And the reason I feel this way is simple: it is because of my religion—my Christianity—that I've learned how to find peace with God, that I understand Him more. It's because of my religion that my relationship with my Creator has been strengthened, my mind expanded, my knowledge increased. It's because of my Christianity that I worship among a community of like-minded believers, and that I know—and fully appreciate—the awesomeness of the Almighty.

Religion is the framework for developing a relationship with Him.

True religion produces right relationship to God which leads to right experience and right intimate relationship with God.
—Gregory Koukl

Rules of Engagement

It seems like everything in this life comes with a set of rules, doesn't it? *Do this, don't do that. Follow this. Don't follow that.* Whether it's the roads we drive on, the country in which we live, the places we work, or the schools we attend, we're inundated with rules in every aspect of our lives—one right after another.

> *The church isn't meant to satisfy our longings. It's meant for messed-up believers to move toward love, unity, and a deep hunger for Jesus.*
> **—Caleb Breakey**

We get beaten over the head with what's required of us—what we must conform to. Rule after rule, we've got to obey. And because of this, many of us have rebelled. Some of us have flat-out resisted. When it comes to following the rules God has set in place, a number of us have boycotted because adhering to a bunch of laws with no understanding as to why we're following them can seem pretty pointless. I mean, we don't want to be the sheep aimlessly following the herd, right? Instead, we want answers to our questions, and if we're forced to follow a rule, we'd better know the purpose in doing so . . . the reason why.

But you're not the only one that feels this way.

Friend, you're not alone . . . not by a long shot.

The Bible is filled with acts of defiance and disobedience toward God—men and women who flat-out rejected His laws. Take Moses and the Israelites, for example. After receiving the Ten Commandments from God, Moses descended from Mount Sinai to deliver the news to His people, only to find them worshipping a golden calf they had constructed from personal possessions—another god. They were unsure of their leader (Moses), tired of waiting on him—tired of waiting on the Lord—and decided to take matters into their own hands. They wanted to take back control.

Um, you can imagine how well this went over with Moses, right?

And God?

Talk about being busted!

Right there in Moses' grip were the Ten Commandments, spoken by God Himself to His people and they'd already broken the first rule: *You shall worship no other gods but me.* They had taken it upon their impatient selves to build an altar and defy the Lord. (The story of the Israelites building the golden calf is found in Exodus 32.)

Whoa.

> *You must have peace with God before you can have the peace of God, and there's a profound difference.*
> **—Gregory Koukl**

Girls, when it comes to God telling us how we should live our lives, maybe it's time we stop seeing the Lord's commands as an inconvenience . . . a set of rules we're *forced* to obey. Now might just be the time to end the protest and leave the picket line for good.

Because God's in control, not us. He makes the rules, and He's got this life of ours in His hands. As hard as it might sometimes be, we must submit to the Lord and His authority.

We must surrender.

TESTIMONY

The Heart of the Matter
Natalie Chambers Snapp

There have been men before . . . who got so interested in proving the existence of God that they came to care nothing for God himself . . . as if the good Lord had nothing to do but to exist. There have been some who were so preoccupied with spreading Christianity that they never gave a thought to Christ.
—**C. S. Lewis**

When I was a new believer, I was hungry to learn as much about Jesus as I possibly could. I wanted to enroll in every Bible study my church offered. I read books by popular Christian authors. I studied Scripture. I diligently read the notes in my study Bible.

I was on the fast track because I thought I needed to make up for lost time—I didn't become a believer until the age of twenty-seven. I felt like everyone around me knew more about what it meant to be a Christian than I did. They knew what to say, how to act, what to believe, and what was "acceptable."

After researching Jesus for a few years, I began to make connections within Scripture and found the truths echoing in my head in various situations. Then it hit me: Jesus was real. And He still IS real. If He still IS real, then why don't I know Him very well?

Sure, I knew all about His miracles. I memorized many of His teachings. I knew the history surrounding biblical times. My head knowledge was solid but my heart knowledge, the one where an authentic relationship with Jesus develops, was sorely lacking.

I prayed in rote, predictable sentences. I didn't stop to thank Him as often as I should have. I often ignored nudges from the Holy Spirit. I had an elementary understanding of obedience. I thought Christian music was too syrupy sweet for me so I didn't listen. In fact, there was a lot I didn't listen to.

Jesus is oftentimes portrayed as a gentle, quiet man who loved everyone—and He was. However, He was also capable of getting angry. Not the kind of angry I get when my kids can't find their shoes and we're already late, but anger directed to those who practiced disobedience or disrespect to God. Most of Jesus' anger was directed at a sect of Jewish teachers called the Pharisees.

The Pharisees preferred rules over grace. They prioritized procedures over people, focused upon what others should be doing, and denounced the sin of others—even though they too were guilty of sin. Legalism was birthed through the Pharisees.

Have you ever heard the story about Jesus healing the man with a crippled hand on the Sabbath? Sure enough, it was the Pharisees who focused on Jesus' choice to heal on the Sabbath rather than on the love and compassion that was bestowed upon this man when he was healed. In fact, Jesus warns the commoners, "Watch out for the teachers of the law. They like to walk around in flowing robes and be greeted with respect in the marketplaces, and have the most important seats in the synagogues and the places of honor at banquets. They devour widows' houses and for a show make lengthy prayers. These men will be punished most severely" (Mark 12:38–40).

The Pharisees had a head relationship with God but they didn't possess much of a heart relationship with Him. They sure could put on a good show but the great commandments of loving God above all else and loving our neighbors as ourselves were lost on them. They were wolves in sheep's clothing (Matt. 7:15).

It's no mystery—God doesn't want to have a head relationship with us. He wants our hearts. In fact, He says in Proverbs 23:26: "My son, give me your heart and let your eyes delight in my ways." He already knows us better than we know ourselves, but relationships can only exist if both parties are involved. If only one is doing the work, the relationship won't ever reach its full potential.

How can you form a heart relationship with Jesus?

Talk to Him. Yes! Pray! God knows the desires of our hearts even before we speak them—but He wants to hear it from us. You can't have a relationship with someone without dialogue, right? If praying is new for you, keep at it—the more you talk to Him, the more open you will be to His responses. You will also begin to recognize the Holy Spirit alive in you!

Keep a prayer journal. Keeping a record of your prayers and how they were fulfilled can solidify your trust in Him and will exhibit the power of prayer.

Listen to worship music. I mentioned I once thought Christian music was too "syrupy sweet" for me, right? Turns out, I was wrong. There is great Christian music available these days. Groups like Bethel Live, Jesus Culture, and Brian and Jenn Johnson are filled with words and melodies that move my soul. There are many genres of Christian music, so finding something you enjoy won't be a challenge.

Be grateful. When we are thankful in all circumstances for what we have, we strengthen our relationship with God. He has provided all of the good and He will make beauty from ashes when the bad comes along. Not to mention, a heart filled with gratitude is the difference between an optimist and a pessimist, and who wants to be a pessimist?

Share your story with others. Revelation 12:11 says "And they overcame him because of the blood of the Lamb and because of the word of their testimony" (NASB). There is power in our own stories, friend. The words of our testimonies can be just the story another person needs to hear to "seal the deal" in accepting Jesus. The more I share my own story, the more in awe of Him I am.

It's easy to look the part of a good Christian, isn't it? If we know enough Scripture, go to enough Bible studies, serve in the community, and attend church each Sunday, then we look like we know God really well, don't we?

However, it's entirely possible to do all of the above and not really know Jesus at all. Apparently, this has been an age-old challenge because Jesus spoke of it in Matthew 7:21–23, saying,

> Not everyone who says to me, "Lord, Lord," will enter the kingdom of heaven, but only the one who does the will of my Father who is in heaven. Many will say to me on that day, "Lord, Lord, did we not prophesy in your name and in your name drive out demons and in your name perform many miracles?" Then I will tell them plainly, "I never knew you. Away from me, you evildoers!"

I know it sounds harsh, but no one likes an imposter.

Jesus wants all of you. He wants you to understand Scripture and learn more about His ways but He doesn't want you to stop there. He wants your heart, too. He wants you to cling to Him when things get tough and He wants you to praise Him when life is good. He cares for you. He wants to be in relationship with you.

He loves you—and He wants you to love Him back.

Girls, don't get caught up in this whole relationship versus religion thing. Because honestly, we need both, don't we? They go hand in hand. We need a community of believers to circle around us, a church to call home, a faith that's on fire, and a meaningful connection with our Creator.

Relationship without religion is just a friendship, but religion without a relationship is just a bunch of rules.
—Paul Mondragon

Prescription for Praise

▐▩➤ READ:

Called to Stay by Caleb Breakey
The Screwtape Letters by C. S. Lewis
God is Able by Priscilla Shirer
Jesus>Religion by Jefferson Bethke

▐▩➤ STUDY:

Psalm 3:3
Deuteronomy 10:12
James 1:27
Micah 6:8
Ecclesiastes 12:13
Romans 1:25
1 Corinthians 11:1–2
1 Peter 1:14–16

▐▩➤ SING:

"With Everything" performed by Hillsong United
"Our God is Greater" performed by Chris Tomlin
"Your Love Never Fails" performed by Jesus Culture
"Overcomer" performed by Mandisa
"I Have Decided" performed by Starfield

APPLY:

1. How do relationship and religion intertwine?

_____

_____

2. What obstacle(s) have you encountered in forming a relationship with God? Explain.

_____

_____

3. Identify the distractions in your life right now. List them here:

_____

_____

4. What can you do to reduce those distractions (the squirrels of this world)? How can you learn to maintain focus while working on a relationship with the Lord? What can you commit to?

_____

_____

5. When it comes to obedience to God, have you found yourself resisting? Boycotting maybe? Why do you think this is?

_____

_____

Blessed is the one who trusts in the LORD, who does not look to the proud, to those who turn aside to false gods.
—Psalm 40:4

CHAPTER 10

Following the Leader

Following Christ isn't something that can be done halfheartedly or on the side. It is not a label we can display when it is useful. It must be central to everything we do and are.

—Francis Chan

Did you read the above quote? I mean *really* read it?

It's powerful, girls. It's convicting. And it can't help but make each one of us think. Am I right?

Believe me when I tell you that I've been found guilty (there's that word again), with a capital *G*, of halfheartedly following Jesus on occasion. There have been times when I've branded myself a follower but haven't walked the walk. Moments when I've been ugly on the inside, hypocritical, and, yes, judgmental, too. Instances where submitting to the Lord has looked pretty pitiful and totally pathetic. And chances are those times I'm least proud of are going to surface again.

It's not easy being a Christian woman. Try as I might, I'm not always the person Jesus calls me to be and, honestly, sometimes I'm not anywhere close. I struggle. I sin. I make choices without consulting God first. And it's in those moments when following the leader—following Christ—looks like anything but.

Wearing the label is a cinch, but living the life God calls us to, and obeying His Word—that takes some effort.

So what's my problem? Better yet—what's *our* problem?

Setting a Foundation

> *Only God can truly fill that lonely place inside you . . . let Him.*
> **—Carey Scott**

Growing up, I knew the difference between right and wrong. I had my morals pretty well set in place, and considered myself as having a decent head on my shoulders, too. I was driven, and knew the direction I wanted to take in life. However, the choices I made never included God. He wasn't in the picture, wasn't one I consulted or thought about on a daily basis, and by no means was *He* the foundation of *my* life.

Not at all.

Things worked well like this for a while (so I thought). Everything was going smoothly—as planned, you could say. God was in His place and I was in mine. I was on my own, independent, and in control. Life was perfect . . . until it wasn't.

The one thing I failed to realize was my journey—everyone's journey in fact—never stays consistent, stable, or constant. Our paths are destined to wind, just as the road we're treading will in fact curve—when we least expect it to. We'll encounter numerous bumps along the way, possibly a collision or two . . . maybe even a dead end.

And it's then, in those painful moments of uncertainty, when we finally turn to God. Right there, in the midst of our troubles is where His Word brings clarity to our troubled souls . . . where His Almighty presence is indeed, tangible.

But it's not as if He hasn't been trying to get our attention, is it? It's not like God hasn't attempted to make Himself known either. Personally speaking, there have been plenty of instances where the Lord sought my heart—moments when He was trying to reach me before the Enemy did. But I didn't listen. Hard times ensued and the regrets I once had the pleasure of never knowing found their way into my life. My weaknesses were preyed upon, my vulnerability exposed. The person and the reputation I had once held dear were no longer. I found myself under attack and in need of a Savior.

It appeared that the Enemy could take a girl with the best intentions (me) and convince her to fall victim in a way she'd never thought possible. And all this took place because Jesus wasn't the center of my life. He wasn't my foundation. Our relationship had yet to be established . . . and I was suffering terribly because of it, and all of those mistakes I was making.

Friend, do you mind if I ask you a question? I know, I know, I've asked a lot of them thus far, but tell me, what would happen if you made a statement right now, and claimed out loud, in a clear and audible voice, "God, I need you"? What if you professed with your entire being that indeed, you desired a Savior—someone else to lean on and trust in in order to get through this life and beyond? Would it make you weaker? Would you feel silly? Maybe a tad awkward? Or would it be freeing? Would your strength double in size? Might you feel less alone and more secure?

You see, the young woman I developed into wasn't ready for what life would throw her way. I couldn't handle situations that varied from my norm because I didn't have God at my core. And believe me when I tell you that right and wrong often get skewed when you're not equipped to handle such battles—when you're living this life separate from Christ. When you don't have a firm foothold in your faith, and when you're ill-prepared for spiritual warfare, the Enemy can persuade you into thinking your lack of judgment is okay, good even.

> *But in your hearts revere Christ as Lord. Always be prepared to give an answer to everyone who asks you to give the reason for the hope that you have.*
> **—1 Peter 3:15**

And it's in that moment that he takes aim.

Girls, each of us may be different, our journeys varied, but one thing is for certain: our foundation must reside in Christ, because if you and I don't stand for something, we'll most likely fall for anything. Amen?

Jesus is our rock. The Lord is our refuge. Seek Them.

I Will Follow Him

> *Right now counts forever.*
> **—R. C. Sproul**

When I think about the modern-day comforts I enjoy as a follower of Christ, I can't help but reflect on biblical times. Call me crazy (or don't), but my mind redirects my thinking back to those days of the apostles. That's right; I start mulling over the life and times of these twelve guys—the men who followed Jesus. They were His tribe, His people—His disciples—and the lives they led were anything *but* comfortable. It was hard. There were plenty of trials combined with loads of uncertainty, too. Yet they kept their faith strong, their hope secured, and their focus centered on their teacher (well, except for Judas, that is [Luke 22:2–6]).

Fast-forward two thousand plus years and here we are: a collective group of women who, for the most part, enjoy the luxuries this blessed life offers. We're able to sit down, with our feet propped up, eating a tub of ice cream (I could seriously

> *God often reinforces our faith after we trust Him, not before.*
> **—Ravi Zacharias**

polish off a gallon of Rocky Road myself right now), watching a reality television show—and yet we're kind of clueless as to why the purpose we're desiring for our lives has yet to be revealed. Or why the connection we seek to have with God isn't deeper . . . more meaningful.

It's as if we're going about life halfway: living for the moment . . . living for ourselves. And it's all because we haven't fully surrendered to Him.

But like the first disciples of Christ, our Father will continually push us in a better direction, just as following Him will lead us to places we never perceived possible. Because the Lord can take the sedentary desire we have for our lives and work it for good. He can use each and every one of us to further His work in His kingdom. But here's the thing: following Him is up to us. It's our decision. It's by our own free will that we readily listen for His voice, submit to His authority, and act upon His call.

I've said it before and I'll say it again: we're not meant to live this life comfortably, and yet so many of us crave this sort of security. I know I have in the past. And still do. But what if you and I chose to sacrifice more of our inner comforts the way

> *Teach me to do your will, for you are my God. May your gracious Spirit lead me forward on a firm footing.*
> **—Psalm 143:10** NLT

the apostles did? No, seriously. What if I told you that the safety we desire and the comfort we long for can be found in following Him? Hey, many of Christ's early disciples had reservations at first, too. Some were skeptical of Jesus and who He proclaimed to be, and why He was calling upon them to follow His lead. Some were just plain uncomfortable. I'll tell you what though: there's never been a more blessed group of guys than the twelve men who willingly ditched it all (like, everything) in order to heed Christ's call. *Blessed*! They got to hang with the Messiah. Right by His side. VIP status! They had the opportunity to live, travel, and serve with the Son of God.

The. Son. Of. God.

Wow.

Now, I'm not naïve. I know that often times, following the leader can be hard. It's a struggle to pay attention, put our opinions aside, and willfully carry out God's plan for our lives . . . especially when we don't always understand it . . . or Him. We don't understand why things happen the way they do. But God does. Just as Jesus has our best interests in mind. And it's the promise of hope He provides (and guarantees) that should be enough. Understanding that the Creator of the Universe and Jesus Christ want nothing but to draw us nearer to Them should be all the proof we need, the reassurance we're hoping for, and the comfort we long to possess. Shouldn't it be the reason to pursue, follow, and place all of our trust in the Lord?

Shouldn't it be the reason we finally surrender?

Indeed, it should.

"Simon says, touch your toes. Simon says, stick out your tongue. Simon says, jump up and down. Now pat your head."

And immediately two or three of your little friends were forced to sit down because they executed a movement without following the correct instructions. They didn't think it through, made a mistake, and got kicked out of the game because of it.

Most of us can recall our first attempts at playing Simon Says. During those elementary days of old, it usually involved an adult (or peer) who stood at the front of the room and then prompted the whole class to mimic his or her gestures.

> *It's in Christ that we find out who we are and what we are living for.*
> **—Ephesians 1:11**
> *The Message*

And as participants in this game, what did we do? Well, we executed those movements and followed directions without any questions as to why. We didn't hesitate either. We trusted and we followed.

Besides, wasn't it rewarding (and just plain fun) to be one of the last ones standing? One of the children who took the time to really listen for the prompts, careful in her actions, mind clear and focused?

Friends, we can do that again.

As I've mentioned (possibly ad nauseam), following the leader can be difficult. But rather than being the kids sidelined for our lack of attention, we need to be the ones still standing . . . the ones still in the game. We've got to tap into what God's trying to tell us and teach us, just as we have to be diligent in avoiding distractions and temptations.

We've got to be willing to follow our leader, and we've got to be eager to comply with His Word.

The Parable of the Lost Son (Luke 15:11–32) tells the story of a young man who, despite all of his teachings, his understanding of the Lord, and the fervent love of his father, decidedly turns his back on it all. He rebels, takes off, wastes his inheritance on wild living, only to find himself in extreme peril once the great famine hits.

Ashamed by his behavior, penniless, and miserable, the son must return home and deal with his family—he must face his sin. But rather than finding a father who's outraged by his poor choices and anxious to disown him for his foolish ways, he stumbles upon a different response instead: forgiveness and grace. He returns to find loving arms that embrace him, and a dad who's overjoyed by his homecoming.

This story oozes unconditional love. I mean, this kid totally blew it, right? He wasted all of his dad's money, left home, ditched his responsibilities, and said "to heck with all of you." And when he returned, tail tucked between his legs, there wasn't even an "I told you so"; nor was there finger-pointing or yelling either. There was only gratitude for his safe return. There was pure joy.

I look at this story of the Prodigal Son and I see a young man who's troubled, rebellious, and completely disobedient. I see a father who is hurt yet compassionate.

I see both of these men and then I see us, too.

Because we've all been disobedient in our lives, haven't we? Whether we've defied our parents, authority in general, or our Father in heaven, we have chosen from time to time (or all the time) to ignore the rules set in place for us. To "unfollow," if you will. We've made mistakes and many of us have felt too ashamed to go back, request forgiveness, or plead for mercy from our God. But just like the father in the story of the Prodigal Son, God is there, waiting with open arms, eager to pardon your sins and rejoice in your homecoming.

No pointing fingers, no yelling, no eye rolls or looks of disgust—God's not about shaming you. He just wants you.

So let's relinquish our desires for control by becoming His followers and trusting in His plan for us. Let's learn to let go and allow God to take over.

Anyone who intends to come with me has to let me lead.
You're not in the driver's seat; I am. Don't run from suffering;
embrace it. Follow me and I'll show you how.
—**Matthew 16:24** *The Message*

 **TESTIMONY**

Outta Control
Carey Scott

I'm a self-professed control freak with deep trust issues, and there are good reasons. Beginning at the innocent age of four, I suffered abuses of every kind that continued well into my adult life. And because I never felt that what I needed was important or valued, I decided that the only person to protect me . . . was me. So I intentionally built protective barriers around my heart and my life, hoping to never be victimized again.

Hey, I like to keep things interesting.

Anyone who experiences abuse has a tendency to try to control the world around them. They want to be in charge so they can stay safe, but in reality it closes them off from really living.

I didn't have roommates because I wanted to control who could visit my apartment. I always drove my car to meet friends so I could leave when I was ready to go. In public places, I'd scan the room to determine the quickest escape route.

My relationships suffered, too. I operated with a strict "one strike and you're out" policy, leaving many good-intentioned people confused and wounded. As much as I wanted to love and be loved, I was scared to

204 · · · For the Love of God

be hurt again and so I ended friendships and dating relationships at the first sign of trouble.

My family was at a loss to know how to help me. I'd ask for help, but then struggle to accept it for fear of any strings that might be attached. I most certainly didn't want to give them any power over me. Being a mom myself, I can't imagine how painful it must have been for my parents to watch me flounder, knowing they couldn't rescue me from myself.

After years of controlling every interaction and every situation, I found myself weary, joyless, and lonely. I knew I was a good person, but my need to manipulate and dominate was weighing me down. My heart longed to be known and cherished, but I didn't want to be hurt again. I tried to mask my broken heart with men, alcohol, food, and anything else that might offer comfort. But it never lasted for long.

Those were some of my darkest days.

The Enemy of your soul lies to you any chance he gets. Do you realize how much he hates you? Since he cannot destroy God, the devil goes after what is closest to His heart: you . . . and me. God's children are on the Enemy's hit list, and one of the greatest lies he tells us is that we have to take care of ourselves.

When we accept that lie as our truth, we are essentially telling God we don't think He can do His job. Rather than ask for His protection, we go rogue and try to control everyone and everything around us. For most of my life, I truly believed I was my sole protector and I had to figure it all out.

But then I collided with this verse: "Trust GOD from the bottom of your heart; don't try to figure out everything on your own. Listen for GOD's voice in everything you do, everywhere you go; He's the one who will keep you on track. Don't assume that you know it all" (Prov. 3:5–6 *The Message*). And it slapped me across the face—in a good way.

These words resonated so deeply, because I realized I'd spent most of my life trying to keep myself on the right track by controlling my world. I didn't listen for God's voice or ask Him for the path He wanted me to follow, because I was convinced He couldn't help me—or would choose not to.

I assumed I knew what was best for me.

But this verse gave me a different understanding of God. Rather than being a distant deity that was powerless to help, I realized He was fully aware of all things . . . including me. He was trustworthy. And most of all, I didn't have to control everything because God had my best interest in mind.

Jeremiah 29:11 confirms this: "I know what I'm doing. I have it all planned out—plans to take care of you, not abandon you, plans to give you the future you hope for" (*The Message*).

He saw me in my human condition—messy, nasty, broken, selfish, bitter, angry, prideful—and loved me anyway. He knew the pain in my heart and the hopelessness inside. He watched me try to make my life manageable in my own strength, and fail. God saw it all—my wandering, my weakness, my wounding. And when I cried out in desperation, He was there.

I'm still bent toward wanting to control the things in my life. I have opinions on how things need to work in my family. I like my kids to behave a certain way. I want my husband to do the things I want him to do . . . when I want them done. I have expectations of my friends, some unrealistic. But I am quicker to step back and let God be God, and realize that I am not.

At least most of the time.

Facing Persecution

"Carry on, Christian Soldier"

Prior to becoming a Christian, I had no clue.

I mean, *how* could I know?

Better yet, *why* didn't I know?

I wasn't aware of what was taking place in neighboring countries and abroad. Nope. No one ever told me that following Christ could in fact cost people their lives (yes, you heard me right!). So as I sat in the sanctuary of my church one evening and watched a documentary on the persecuted church, I grew painfully aware of what this world thinks of Christians and Christianity as a whole, as well as their thoughts on Jesus.

And what I saw left me speechless.

Please know I don't say this to scare you. My job isn't to freak you out on the very idea of practicing Christianity, but I think you need to be made aware, because there are so many countries in this great big world we inhabit where people are unable to worship as they see fit. They can't profess Christ's name or praise Him in public. They aren't allowed to seek their Savior, to disciple to others, or experience basic religious freedoms. Others with different demographics don't share the faith-based luxuries we do.

They're not allowed to follow God.

And it appears there are a number of places in this world where following Christ is considered a crime.

> For whoever wants to save their life will lose it, but whoever loses their life for me and for the gospel will save it.
> —**Mark 8:35**

I was surprised, too. In shock you could say.

After learning this information, and upon witnessing the graphic images displayed before me on the screen that night, my heart began to ache. My anxiety tripled as I thought about the suffering taking place halfway around the world. And as I became aware of these plights, my stomach began to churn.

However, persecution against Christians is nothing new.

People put on trial, treated like criminals for living their faith out loud, and even put to death for believing in Jesus. Troubling, isn't it? But it's been happening for ages. Throughout history, millions have been mistreated for preaching the Word of God and the teachings of Christ. Need examples? Look no further than the Bible. Peter was thrown out of town (and later crucified) for being a disciple of Jesus. How about John the Baptist, Saul of Tarsus? Oh, and what about Stephen, who was one of the first to be murdered for his beliefs after Christ's resurrection (34 AD)? And all of the apostles (with the exception of John)? Each of these men were murdered for their faith. And that's just during biblical times.

It continues today.

You know, if you had asked me this question a few years back, I would have told you that the days of religious persecution were long gone. I would have believed it, too. But it's just not the case. We are indeed a persecuted church. Instance after instance in our present-day world continues to support my claim.

Hold up. How can this be happening, you ask.

Christians have been slain in other countries for having the same faith you're striving to obtain. Jailed, imprisoned, tortured— all for loving our God and His Son who saved us.

Still, they go. Missionaries flock to countries where religious persecution takes place. They hand out Bibles, teach about Christ, spread hope in the most dire of situations, and they do so at a risk.

Can you imagine? Better yet—can you appreciate the freedom and sheer blessing it is to study His Word without fear of condemnation? Don't let it go to waste. Pick up your Bible, friend, read His words, apply His teachings . . . and follow Him.

Follow Christ because you've been blessed with the freedom to do so.

What Would Jesus Do?

> *We need our reality to meet our theology.*
> **—Beth Moore**

To be honest, I don't know how Jesus did it.

I don't know how He was able to love others like He did. I'm not sure how He retained compassion for those who spat in His face. I'm dumbfounded by His ability to pray for those responsible for His death. And I haven't a clue as to what it would look like to love a murderer or embrace a thief. But Jesus does.

Jesus did.

For you and me, loving the unlovable can seem slightly impossible, right? Uncomfortable even. But haven't we all been deemed unlovable at some point in our lives? Whether it's a poor decision we've made, a harmful act we've committed, or the unkind words we've spoken (the ones we wish we could take back), it appears we're not used to the idea of unconditional love because our surroundings have demonstrated how conditional love can be.

Mess up here—pay the price. Make a mistake? Your friendship's over. Say something wrong; get judged. One condition after another is what we've experienced. Worse? Many of us are unfamiliar with the grace and forgiveness God bestows, because we've allowed the noise of this world to rise up and tell us otherwise.

Following the leader? Following Christ? Friends, I'm going to tell you right now that it's going to take some sacrifice. Why? Because it requires selflessness. It means serving all cultures and all people, it's walking the walk, and it's ditching the desires of this world all in pursuit of the next.

Following Christ means considering Jesus—it's thinking about what He would do, how He would act, and what He might say in every situation we encounter.

By calling these men to leave their boats, Jesus was call-ing them to abandon their careers. When He called them to leave their nets, He was calling them to abandon their possessions. When He called them to leave their father in the boat by himself, He was calling them to abandon their family and friends. Ultimately, Jesus was calling them to abandon themselves. (David Platt)[1]

Jesus called upon His disciples by asking them to die to them-selves, ditch their possessions, and everything else they knew in order to follow His lead. He's asking us to do the same. He's asking us to follow Him, too.

All that matters is the reality of who we are before God.
—Francis Chan

Prescription for Praise

 **READ:**

Follow Me by David Platt
Not a Fan by Kyle Idleman
Let Hope In by Pete Wilson
Multiply by Francis Chan
Wonderstruck by Margaret Feinberg

STUDY:

1 Peter 2:21
1 John 2:3–4
Matthew 16:24

Matthew 7:21–23
Luke 9:23
Matthew 4:19–25
1 Timothy 4:11–16
Psalm 51:10
2 John 1:6
John 3:16

SING:

"I Will Follow" performed by Chris Tomlin
"Tell the World" performed by Lecrae
"In Better Hands" performed by Natalie Grant
"You Are For Me" performed by Kari Jobe
"Blessings" by Laura Story

APPLY:

1. What does following Jesus look like to you? What actions can one take to do just that?

_____

_____

2. I discussed the persecuted church in this chapter. How has this changed your idea of what serving God looks like? What does it mean to serve at all costs?

_____

_____

3. As you look at your life right now, what small changes can you make in order to consider God more, and yourself less? What ideas do you have when it comes to focusing more on Him?

_____

_____

4. Carey Scott talked about losing the need for control and what that really means. Have you struggled with this issue? If so, how did her words help you?

_____

_____

5. Can you think of an instance where thinking more like Christ could have made a big difference? Where a different outcome may have resulted if you'd seen the situation through His eyes? Explain.

_____

_____

Just put your faith in God and one day you'll see.
—Lenny Kravitz

Note:
1   David Platt, "What It Means to Follow Christ," Lifeway, accessed March 31, 2014, http://www.lifeway.com/Article/christian-living-what-it-means-to-follow-christ.

CHAPTER 11

What's Next?

If you perform your part, God will fulfill His.

—Watchman Nee

So, what's next?

It's a good question, you know.

Now that we've reached the end of this guide, it's an uncertainty you're left to consider. Where do you go from here, what plan of action follows, and, seriously, what are *you* going to do next?

I could go ahead and outline the individual steps you need to take in order to further your spiritual efforts and your relationship with God. I'm well aware of the path you must tread . . . the walk you must commit to . . . the choice you *should* make. The thing is—girls, this isn't *my* decision. It's yours. And the next step in your walk, well, it's completely up to you.

Now, you can choose to disregard everything you've read. You can take the information I've provided and totally discount

213

it. You can size me up as just another brainwashed Bible thumper caught up in the Word . . . or you can resolve to learn more—to experience firsthand the love of Jesus and, yes, the glory of God.

I'm not one to push, but honestly, why bother sitting on that fence any longer? Why fret over which way to go, or what direction to turn? Why waste another minute second-guessing God and His plans for you?

The time has come.

And just like that he was gone.

It was a hot July afternoon. The type of summer day where the sun seemingly kisses the sky into a crisp shade of blue. The kind of day one reflects upon in the midst of winter's harshness. And it was on this day that I learned about the sudden (and unexpected) passing of Taylor Wood. If you're attempting to pick your brain as to who this might be, allow me to inform you that he wasn't a celebrity. He wasn't a famous athlete either. Taylor was a regular guy, newly married, with his whole life in front of him. And he knew Jesus was the answer.

But as he joined friends at a local river that summer afternoon, Taylor's life came to an abrupt end. In an instant, he had slipped from this life to the next . . . and safely into the arms of Jesus.

He was just twenty-three years old.

We've heard stories like this before, right? A soul plucked too soon from this earth. A loved one unexpectedly taken well before their time. Yet when these things happen, it only adds to our confusion. Tragedies like these leave us puzzled by their occurrence. We feel sympathy and grief, anger and sadness. We hurt for those affected. And then? Then we direct our attention to ourselves. In those moments after another's life has passed, our thoughts can't help but wander to our own mortality, as we contemplate *our* eternity.

But the reason I tell this story? It has to do with Taylor's family, and, more specifically, his mother's example of unshakeable faith. Just one day after her son's passing, Taylor's mom proceeded to update her status on Facebook . . . and her words are some I'll never forget. I wept for her loss. But I sobbed uncontrollably after seeing the strength she displayed, the trust she maintained, and the praise she willingly offered up to God in her most difficult hour. You see, it was through her son's death, that she became a witness to his life and that of his Savior.

This is what she said:

> We went to the river tonight for a special time of honoring Taylor and to see where he took his last breath. It was a beautiful fun spot that did not look dangerous at all. Even me, chicken Mama, would have swam there. God chose for Taylor to start his new spin on eternity right there. It was no mistake but a pure-ordained-God-planned-ushering-into-heaven moment. As we sang "How Great is Our God," prayed, lit candles, threw flowers, and wrote on the amazing steel cross Taylor's friends made, we looked up to see a beautiful full moon. It was just like the one God gave us last month at his wedding . . .

How many of us could endure such pain, such loss, and in that very moment of immense grief, turn around and thank God for His goodness? How many of us could venture down to the spot where our child (or loved one) passed away and begin worshipping God . . . offering praise? That is genuine faith, friends. True devotion.

Girls, it's everything!

Taylor's passing taught me so much, but it was his mother's faith that spoke volumes about the God we love and her relationship with Him. It was in her pain that she took the focus away from her grief by glorifying her Creator instead.

I know this is going to sound cliché, and you might just roll your eyes in response to this next question, but I'm going to go ahead and ask it anyway. Tell me, friends, if your days were numbered, if your life were to soon pass—tell me, what would you do differently? How would this exact moment change? Hear me out by considering the possibility of what I'm asking here. How would you deal? What would you do? Would your eternity come into focus? Would you be more concerned with the afterlife, as well as the state of your spirituality? And if so, then why can't we do that right now? Why can't we concentrate on what really matters and let the world in all its busyness and confusion remain out of sight?

Why can't we surrender to Jesus?

> *My son, give me your heart, and let your eyes observe my ways.*
> **—Proverbs 23:26 ESV**

It's a choice only you can make . . . one you must arrive at all on your own. But He is waiting, girls . . . for that wall to come down, the guard to fall, and for that heart of yours to become His. God's been patiently standing by for you to hand it all over—those struggles, that pain, those issues, your past. He's waiting for you to surrender . . . to come out with your hands up, your heart willing, and your sights set on Him.

Sweet Surrender

As I've told you from the beginning, it's not by chance, nor is it some type of coincidence that this book landed in your hands at this time in your life. It's yet another example of God at work—calling upon you, asking for your return, wanting *you* to know Him better—wanting to bless you, friend, more than you can possibly imagine.

> And now, just as you accepted Christ Jesus as your Lord, you must continue to follow him. Let your roots grow down into him, and let your lives be built on him. Then your faith will grow strong in the truth you were taught, and you will overflow with thankfulness. (Col. 2:6–7 NLT)

It's true.

God is at work in every single one of us, all the time. Throughout the course of writing this book, He's been working on me, too. This doesn't come as any surprise. Considering the scope and magnitude of a project such as this, God's going to reveal many things. It's a given. And wouldn't you know it, halfway through compiling this manuscript, I felt a gentle tug—a nudge, if you will. It was in that stillness, as I waited for God's revelation, that I understood exactly what He was up to—what He was calling His child (me) to do.

Like you, He was asking for *my* complete surrender . . . for my undivided attention and my whole heart. Girls, He was asking me to be baptized in His name.

The thing is, I'd been baptized before. Long ago, that cool water passed over my head well before I knew what it meant or had a say in any of it. And now? Now it was time for me to knowingly accept my salvation and proclaim my belief in God and His Son—on my own and by my free will.

So as I slipped on that white robe, as I walked into the reservoir filled with water—my children watching in the wings—I professed with my whole heart my desire to be His, to walk with Him, to live

> *Whoever believes and is baptized will be saved.*
> **—Mark 16:16a**

for His kingdom, and to stake my claim as His girl. As my pastor plunged me into that water, my past was washed away. Just like that. And I emerged brand new. I was free. Pure.

I. Was. His. And I had surrendered.

Reflecting upon that moment, Matthew 3:16–17 comes to mind. It's a passage that finds Jesus and John the Baptist together in the Jordan River. John has just been asked to baptize the Messiah. Wrapped up in his own self-doubts and feelings of unworthiness, John tells the Son of God no (could you imagine). He couldn't process the enormity of such a request, so it was easier for him to decline this invitation than to accept such an honor. But Jesus knew better and as John immersed Christ into the river, the Savior emerged, "heaven was opened, and he saw the Spirit of God descending like a dove and alighting on him. And a voice from heaven said, 'This is my Son, whom I love; with him I am well pleased.'"

Well pleased. I like to think of my baptism—my surrender—and know that for my act of obedience, God was well pleased. For my acceptance of salvation, repentance from past sins, and the embrace of the Word that came into play that day, God was pretty proud of His kid.

And you know what? When it comes to seeking our Creator, developing a relationship, and loving others how He's called us to . . . He's proud of us all.

Vapors and Such

In writing this book, there have been a number of times when I've wanted to stop. Times when I wanted to shut down the computer, step back from my desk, and turn away from this manuscript. Doubts festered as I couldn't help but question my ability to pen this thing—second-guessing myself over and over again. I felt overwhelmed by the pressure to deliver exactly what you (the reader) are in need of—unbelievable pressure to write that which stirs your soul and redirects your path . . . a book that draws you closer to an understanding of God . . . nearer to Him. I've feared what critics might say, what scholars might write about my efforts, and I've listened to the Enemy trick me into thinking not a single soul will benefit from its message. That I am, in fact, wasting my time.

However, there's this rule in the publishing industry . . . a piece of advice that writers are encouraged to follow, one that I held fast to in the crafting of these words, and it goes a little something like this: *write what you know*. Well girls, this book and the contents within are exactly that—what I know. Because it's my own experiences with uncertainty and doubt that led me on this journey. It's my own struggles in living a life separate from Christ that pushed me to pursue a relationship with Him in the first place. I understand what it's like to be new to the faith, lost in church, and envious of believers who seemingly possess more biblical knowledge than I. I'm fully aware of the shame that accompanies one's past, and the anxious desire to hide it from others. I understand this, just as I understand you too, friend.

I've been you.

I *am* you.

The message I've shared and my goal in doing so has been to change the way you look at everything . . . not just the way you see yourself and this life you're living, but the environment that surrounds you, and the Creator who made you. So, take this newfound sight—this information you've been given—and fix your eyes upon Jesus.

For this life is but a vapor.

I don't say this to scare you. I don't tell you such a thing to push you away. Rather, it's to help you realize there's a sense of urgency as I type these words. It's true. None of us is guaranteed tomorrow. Not the next hour, not the next minute, not even the next breath. And even though we're aware of this—even though we recognize how temporary the lives we lead are—we live as though they're not.

> *I can't tell you how much I long for you to enter this*
> *wide-open, spacious life. We didn't fence you in. The smallness*
> *you feel comes from within you. Your lives aren't small,*
> *but you're living them in a small way. I'm speaking*
> *as plainly as I can and with great affection.*
> *Open up your lives. Live openly and expansively!*
> **—2 Corinthians 6:11–13** *The Message*

Hey, mind if I ask you one more favor (you know, before our time together ends)? Girls, I want you to think about the state of your life right now. I want you to take a moment, close your eyes, and attempt to really grasp the hours, the minutes, and even the seconds laid out before you in a given day (I have a point in asking this, I swear). You see, each morning we rise, we start over—fresh, if you will. Every twenty-four hours we have yet another chance to change. To live life differently . . . to push the reset button, to wipe the slate clean. Each and every day we have the opportunity to start our lives over in Christ.

But what happens instead?

Our days usually find us heading off to our jobs, tending to our appointments, and marking off items on those to-do lists. It finds us caught up in our own schedules . . . in our chaos. And do we ever really inhale the very breath of life? Do we take in those moments we've been given by realizing the beauty in each one?

My prayer is that you'll continue this walk, keep an open mind to His Word, pursue Christ, seek God, and embrace Christianity. I pray that your thirst for knowledge leads you to more time in His presence . . . that you'll grow confident in your God—your belief in Him—and never let it wane. That you'll go to Him each and every day, seek His glory, serve His people, and revel in His affection.

> *On the average day, we live caught up in ourselves. On the average day, we don't consider God very much. On the average day, we forget that our life truly is a vapor.*
> **—Francis Chan**

My dear friend, your past is gone, the future is now, and the love that God has for you is eternal . . . it's everlasting. You. Are. His.

Seek Him.

Embrace Him.

Trust Him.

Your invitation is here.

His arms are open.

And God is waiting . . . for you.

No eye has seen, no ear has heard, no mind has conceived what God has prepared for those who love him.
—1 Corinthians 2:9 NIV 1984

PART 4

Taking Action

"The Lord God is waiting to show how kind he is and to have pity on you. The Lord always does right; he blesses those who trust him."
—Isaiah 30:18 CEV

Bible Reading Plan

The best way to make your way through the Bible is to begin a Bible-reading plan. Most of these recommendations will guide you through God's Word in about a year, but some vary. Check out the following links and start a plan that works for you.

Online:

Bible Gateway Online Devotion-a-Day: www.biblegateway.com/reading-plans/

Bible Study Tools Online Reading Plans/Newsletter: www.biblestudytools.com/bible-reading-plan/

ESV Bible: about.esvbible.org/resources/reading/

Apps:

YouVersion: www.bible.com (Multiple apps, downloads, and a number of different reading plans are available.)

Olive Tree: www.olivetree.com

Blue Letter Bible: www.blueletterbible.org

Downloads/PDFs:

Ligonier Ministries: www.ligonier.org/blog/bible-reading-plans/

MAPS

Manuscript • Archeological • Prophecies • Statistical

I love this acrostic—MAPS—provided by Dr. Steven Crane of Eagle Christian Church. Here, Dr. Crane breaks down the truth contained in the Bible as well as the accuracy of this book for us:

M: The Bible has unparalleled MANUSCRIPT evidence. There are over twenty-four thousand partial or complete manuscript copies of the New Testament in existence today. With such a wealth of manuscripts, we can be assured of the Bible's accuracy.

A: The Bible has been proven to be historically reliable by numerous ARCHAEOLOGICAL discoveries. To date, more than twenty-five thousand archaeological discoveries have verified the names of persons, places, events, and customs mentioned in the Bible. Open the Bible and you will find real cities, places, and events.

P: The Bible, unlike any other religious book, has demonstrated itself to be the Word of God through its ability to predict the future. There are literally hundreds of very specific PROPHECIES in the Bible that were fulfilled hundreds and even thousands of years after they were spoken.

S: The Bible's accuracy, predictive nature, and archaeological evidence are so amazing that it cannot be STATISTICALLY explained in any other way. For instance, what is the statistical probability that a book which is actually a collection of sixty-six different books written down by more than forty different authors over a period of more than fifteen hundred years on three different continents and in three different languages can contain one central message and one united theme? The Bible remains absolutely consistent and internally harmonious from beginning to end.

Prayer List 911

We've already established that life can be pretty tough at times, right? Here's a list of scriptures to be used when specific issues arise. Take it to prayer, girls. He's listening.

Even better? Download this valuable resource by visiting my website: www.jennyleesulpizio.com.

Confused: Isaiah 40:31; Jeremiah 33:3; Psalm 118:5

Discouraged: Psalm 86:15; Psalm 45:11; Luke 1:37

Doubtful: John 3:16; Isaiah 49:15–16; 1 Corinthians 2:9–10

Pained: Psalm 91:4; Psalm 62:5; Psalm 37:5

Sad: Colossians 3:2; Deuteronomy 3:16; Jeremiah 1:5; Psalm 46:10

Stressed: Jeremiah 29:11; Proverbs 3:5–6; Matthew 6:19–21

Suffering: Job 19:25; Psalm 103:4–5

Worried: Philippians 4:6–7; 2 Timothy 1:7; Isaiah 43:1–2

Serving Others: Christian Charitable Foundations

To serve others is one of the greatest gifts we can give, to those we serve as well as to ourselves. And there are so many amazing and deserving charities we can donate our time and money to. Please, friends, take a few moments to visit the websites of each one of these organizations. Look at the work being done and if you feel called to serve in such a manner—then by all means, please do.

Sole Hope: www.solehope.org

Compassion International: www.compassion.com

Mercy House Kenya: www.mercyhousekenya.org

America World Adoption: www.awaa.org

Tumaini International: www.tumainiinternational.org

Destiny Rescue: www.destinyrescue.org

World Vision: www.worldvision.org

Samaritan's Purse: www.samaritanspurse.org

Tiny Hands International: www.tinyhandsinternational.org

Vi Bella Jewelry: www.vibellajewelry.com

Help One Now: www.helponenow.org

One Simple Wish: www.onesimplewish.org

147 Million Orphans: www.147million.org

End Bible Poverty: www.endbiblepoverty.org

Pure Charity: www.purecharity.com

Church Speak: A Dictionary of Terms

Atonement: Doctrine that describes how you and I can be reconciled to God. It refers to the forgiveness of sins through the price that was paid by Jesus Christ—His death and resurrection—for our salvation. By Jesus suffering vicariously for the sins of humanity, He has taken the punishment due them and given them the opportunity for at-ONE-ment with God.

Born Again: A spiritual new birth. To be saved. Conversion to faith in Christ Jesus as the grounds for God forgiving one's sins.

Bride of Christ: You might be thinking, *"Huh? Um, Jesus wasn't married."* The bride of Christ refers to the church. We are the bride of Christ, His true love, if you will.

Church Home: Where one places their church membership . . . where they attend church on a regular basis. Their chosen community of fellow believers.

Communion (also called the Lord's Supper in some churches): A time of worship in which Christians remember Christ and the sacrifice He made on our behalf by a symbolic reenactment of Jesus' Last Supper with His followers. Participants in Communion share bread and wine (or a non-alcoholic substitute) to represent the body and blood of Christ, given to reconcile us to God. (For a description in Scripture of Jesus giving the bread and wine to His apostles at the Last Supper, see Matt. 26:17–30; Mark 14:12–26; and Luke 22:7–20.)

Doctrine: A teaching and/or set of guiding beliefs. Doctrine is extremely important in Christianity. It defines for us who God is; what He has done; what the Trinity is; the deity of Christ; His resurrection, salvation,

230 · · · For the Love of God

and justification; and all other matters that relate to the actions and beliefs regarding one's relationship with God.

Expository Preaching/Teaching: A style of preaching or teaching that focuses on a particular passage of Scripture, studying it in detail and looking at its meaning in its original context as a method to understand and explain what the Bible means by what it says.

Forgiveness: The act by which one releases the right to hold someone accountable or punishable for hurt or offenses caused by others. Jesus used the Parable of the Unmerciful Servant, recorded in Matthew 18:21–35, to illustrate how we should forgive one another.

Fruit of the Spirit: A biblical term that refers to a list given by Paul to the Galatian church of nine visible traits that mark a true Christian life: love, joy, peace, forbearance, kindness, goodness, faithfulness, gentleness, and self-control (Gal. 5:22–23).

Gospel: The term *gospel*, generally used to refer to the teachings of the Christian religion, simply means "good news." It is the central message of the work of Jesus Christ to unite sinners who are alienated from God to Him. The Apostle Paul, in Romans 1:16, says the gospel is "the power of God that brings salvation to everyone who believes."

Grace: An unconditional gift—no strings attached!—of mercy and love from God to humanity, which we have done nothing to deserve. It is by God's spontaneous, unmerited, loving grace that we are offered salvation through Jesus' death on the cross to pay for our sins.

Hands and Feet of Christ: The acts of service that Christians perform for others on behalf of Christ to exemplify His love.

Holy: Holy means "set apart," dedicated to the service of God; also, regarded with reverence or as worthy of worship.

Inspiration: The word *inspiration* comes from a Latin word meaning "to breathe into." In the religious connotation it means that there is a sense in which God supernaturally conveys the content of a message. Biblical inspiration means God breathed the message of Scripture into the hearts of its writers; it was not just a collection of some "good thoughts" of a few authors. For Christians, inspiration is a gift received from the Holy Spirit to direct and guide us.

Justification: God's act of taking away the guilt and penalty of sin. It is a legal declaration of innocence made possible only by the work of Christ on the cross. A simple way to define this is "just as if I had never sinned." (In the opposite direction, could also be known as "just as if I had always obeyed.")

Nondenominational: A term signifying that a local church congregation is affiliated with no centralized church government or agency that provides structure/doctrine/oversight. Nondenominational churches are self-governed and make their own decisions regarding policy, doctrine, discipline, and other church matters.

Parishioner: A member of a community of gathered people in a church; church member.

Purity: The absence of contamination by sin or guilt. As humans, we don't possess this, "For all have sinned and fall short of the glory of God" (Rom. 3:23). Christians should possess the desire for purity, but due to original sin, no person can achieve purity without God's help.

Repent: To express heartfelt regret or remorse over offending God with our sin; to be more than sorry. Repentance involves a change of one's mind, one's thoughts, and one's behavior toward conformity with God's will/plan for one's life.

Resurrection: Coming back to life after death. To be raised from the dead (spiritually speaking in one aspect, but also physically). Resurrection to live forever with God is the hope of the Christian after life on this earth ends.

Righteousness: The quality of being right or justified in one's actions; acting in accordance with God's law; leading a life that is pleasing to God.

Sabbath: A day set aside each week for rest and worship. As recorded in the book of Genesis, on the seventh day God rested from His labor. "Then God blessed the seventh day and made it holy, because on it he rested from all the work of creating that he had done" (Gen. 2:3). God through Moses instructed the Israelites to "remember the Sabbath day by keeping it holy" (see Ex. 20:8–11).

Salvation: Deliverance from sin and its consequences, made possible by the sacrifice of Jesus Christ on our behalf; being rescued from the righteous judgment of God upon sinners.

Sanctified: The act or process of making something or someone holy, free from sin, or clean before God.

Secular: Attitudes, activities, or other things having no religious or spiritual basis; worldly; not religious.

Spiritual Gifts: Supernatural graces given to individual Christians by the Holy Spirit. Christians need spiritual gifts to fulfill the church's mission.

Tithing: Giving a tenth of one's income to support the church (to God ultimately), as a means of thankfulness and in acknowledgment of what God has granted us through the ability to work and live. May also be known as spiritual giving.

Trinity: One God in three persons: the Father (God), the Son (Jesus Christ), and the Holy Spirit. The three persons are distinct, yet one.

And He Shall Be Called . . .
Free Printable

Feel free to download this printable as my gift to you by visiting my website:

www.jennyleesulpizio.com.

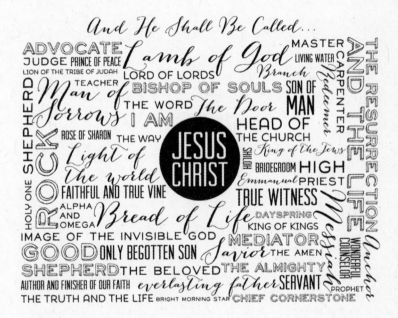

Contributors

Laura S. Cabanillas is an author, conference speaker, licensed mental health counselor, blogger, recovering people pleaser, and a hope whisperer. She lives with her family in Seattle, Washington. To find out more, check out her website at www.voiceofhope. net. You can also find Laura on Facebook and follow her on Twitter @hopewhisperer1.

Hester Christensen is a pastor's wife, mom, author, and speaker. She has served in ministry with her husband for twenty years. Three delightful boys, fourteen, twelve, and nine years old, fill their home with demolition, joy, and lots of entertainment. Hester is a contributing author to *Women in High Def*, and has published work featured in multiple magazines and online sites. She has impacted numerous women in the United States and internationally through retreats, conferences, Bible studies, and other women's events. Her passion is leading women toward spiritual maturity, but her greatest desire is to bring glory to her King. You can find her at HesterChristensen.com.

Kathy Howard helps women live an unshakeable faith for life by encouraging them to stand firm on our rock-solid God no matter the circumstances. Kathy, who has a masters in Christian education, has been teaching the Bible for over twenty-five years. Kathy and her husband have three children, a son-in-law, and one grandson. Find out about her books and speaking ministry and get free discipleship tools and leader helps at: www.kathyhoward.org.

Joanne Kraft is a busy mom and the author of *Just Too Busy: Taking Your Family on a Radical Sabbatical*. A sought-after speaker, Joanne's articles have been published by *Chicken Soup for the Soul*, *Thriving Family*, *In Touch*, *ParentLife*, *Today's Christian Woman*, *P31 Woman*, and more. She's appeared on CBN, *Focus on the Family* and *Family Life Today*. You can find her by visiting www.joannekraft.com.

Jennifer Dukes Lee is the author of *Love Idol: Letting Go of Your Need for Approval—and Seeing Yourself through God's Eyes*. She is a grace dweller and storyteller, and you can find her at www.jenniferdukeslee.com.

Heather R. Riggleman is the author of *Mama Needs a Time-Out*, and frequently speaks to women's groups about marriage and the trenches of motherhood. Known as "The Real Mom," she keeps it real sharing her imperfections about being a hot-tempered wife and mom to three kids on her blog, HeatherRiggleman.com.

Carey Scott is an author, speaker, and life coach who is honest about her walk with the Lord—stumbles, fumbles, and all. Through her ministry, she challenges women to be real—not perfect. She lives in Colorado with her husband and two kids. Learn more about Carey at CareyScottTalks.com.

 **Stephanie Shott** is the founder of The M.O.M. Initiative, a popular international speaker, and author of *The Making of a Mom* and *Ecclesiastes: Understanding What Matters Most*. She has also written articles for various publications and is called upon by media outlets to share her story of adoption, a decade of abuse, and how God makes beauty out of ashes.

 **Natalie Chambers Snapp** is first and foremost a follower of Jesus, then wife to Jason, and mom to one spunky daughter and two spirited sons with a crazy amount of energy. As a later-in-life believer, Natalie is passionate about sharing the grace, mercy, and truth of God's love with a spirit of authenticity through a "get real" approach. She blogs at www.nataliesnapp.com in the free moments between shuttling children and writing the outpourings of her heart. Her first book, *Heart Sisters: Be the Friend You Want to Have*, will be released by Abingdon Press in spring 2015.

 **Tracy Steel** is proudly married to Chad, a pilot in the Air Force. Whenever they are not moving, she loves to drink green tea, chase her young children around the house, and watch reruns of *Lost*. Tracy graduated from Phoenix Seminary in 2005 and served as the Director of Student Women at Scottsdale Bible Church from 2005 to 2007. She is also the author of *Images of His Beauty*, a Bible study for young women who struggle with self-image issues and eating disorders. She currently pursues her passion for ministry via speaking and writing on her blog, One Degree, www.onedegreeministries.com.